MY LAST FLIGHT OUT

Last Pilot Who Escaped After
The Fall Of Viet Nam

CON NGUYEN

Copyright © 2019 Con Nguyen.

All rights reserved. No part of this book may be reproduced, stored, or transmitted by any means—whether auditory, graphic, mechanical, or electronic—without written permission of the author, except in the case of brief excerpts used in critical articles and reviews. Unauthorized reproduction of any part of this work is illegal and is punishable by law.

This book is a work of non-fiction. Unless otherwise noted, the author and the publisher make no explicit guarantees as to the accuracy of the information contained in this book and in some cases, names of people and places have been altered to protect their privacy.

ISBN: 978-1-6847-0697-6 (sc)
ISBN: 978-1-6847-0701-0 (hc)
ISBN: 978-1-6847-0698-3 (e)

Library of Congress Control Number: 2019908733

Because of the dynamic nature of the Internet, any web addresses or links contained in this book may have changed since publication and may no longer be valid. The views expressed in this work are solely those of the author and do not necessarily reflect the views of the publisher, and the publisher hereby disclaims any responsibility for them.

Any people depicted in stock imagery provided by Getty Images are models, and such images are being used for illustrative purposes only.
Certain stock imagery © Getty Images.

Lulu Publishing Services rev. date: 07/23/2019

FOREWORD

"*My Last Flight Out* is an incredible story of selfless military service, leadership, guts, creativity, and perseverance, against overwhelming odds. It's a story worth telling and worth reading."

Rob Campbell
Kenmore, Washington

"For all readers who are interested in true, war memoirs, this book is a ***must-read***. The author, Con Nguyen, flew many different missions and served many positions from the ***beginning to the end*** of the Viet Nam War. His book tells of how he survived - in order to save many, including his *beloved* family. ***My Last Flight Out*** is so *exciting* and *suspenseful* I couldn't put it down. I highly recommend it."

Lanette Davis
Kalua-Kona, Hawaii

ACKNOWLEDGMENTS

Thank you from the bottom of my heart to:

My wife Linda N. Nguyen, my son Steve Nguyen and his wife Hanna, my daughters Trina Schurman and her husband Dave, Susie Schmidley and her husband Michael, Robert Campbell, Lanette Davis and all our friends who supported, encouraged and assisted me in writing this book.

All pilots and crew members of Chinook 249 Squadron. Captain Q. Trong, Captain Nien, Lieutenant Be, Sergeant Son, and special thanks to the members of my Chinook crew in my last flight out on April 30, 1975, with the Chinook tail number "000." Also, I would like to thank all four Chinook crew members under my leadership during the unforgettable evacuation at midnight on April 28, 1975, to Con Son Island.

My friends, my comrades who went through and survived the most dangerous Secret Wars in Viet Nam with the US

Special Operations. Thanks to Thinh, An, Tuong, Trong, De, and many brave crew members of the KingBee pilots from the 219th Squadron.

The brave KingBee pilots of the VNAF 219th Squadron, US Air Force's 20th Special Operations Squadron, the Marine's Scarface, Yellow Jacket and Eagle Claw, the Green Hornet helicopter Gunships, the 101st Airborne Division, the American Division, Air Force forward air-controllers, Vietnamese Air Force A1-E Skyraiders, and many others whose names I may have forgotten.

John Stryker Meyer, *Soldier of Fortune* magazine, American Special Operations Veterans, and all members of the Special Forces who served in the Vietnam War.

"I fought the war we did not start; I finished the war we did not end."

Con Nguyen, *My Last Flight Out*, Chapter 5, Page #64 & 65

"For the American servicemen, it was the thankless war; for the Vietnamese, the war was senseless and destructive to their country."

Con Nguyen, *My Last Flight Out*, Chapter 10 Page# 150

TABLE OF CONTENTS

1. The War Is Over 1
2. The Unexpected Mission 8
3. Miracle And Faith 36
4. Journey On The High Seas 41
5. A Lonely Child 55
6. Poor Family 69
7. National Military Academy Da Lat 74
8. Kingbee Pilots 87
9. Missions Impossible 94
10. More Missions Impossible 121
11. Chinook Operations 153

ABBREVIATIONS

AC	Aircraft Commander
Affirmative	Yes
AK-47	Communist Automatic assault rifle
AR-15	American Automatic assault rifle
AWAC	Airborne Warning and Control
Can bo	Government Official
Cong an	Secret Security
CC	Command and Control
CCC	Control Center of North of SOG
CCN	Control Center of Center of SOG
CCS	Control Center of South of SOG
Cobra	Two-seater attack helicopter
DMZ	Demilitarized Zone
DOA	Defense Office Attaché
FAA	Federal Aviation and Administration
FAC	Forward Air Command

FOB	Forward Operation Base
Gunship	Helicopter armed with machine guns, rockets, grenades
Huey	The nickname of UH1, Utility helicopter
IFR	Instrument Flight Rules
INS	Immigration and Naturalization Service
KingBee	Code name of VNAF 219th Squadron
LZ	Landing Zone
MACV	Military Assistance Command Vietnam
Negative	No
Out	End of the communication
Over	Please respond back (radio communication)
Quan Am	Guanyin refers to Buddhist bodhisattva
Roger	Acknowledge and understood (radio communication)
RT	Reconnaissance Team
RTB	Return to Base
SA7	surface-to-air missiles-Heat seeking
SAM	surface-to-air missiles
SAR	Search and Rescue
SkyRaider	Old propeller fighter Aircraft
SOG	Studies and Observations Group
Spec Ops	Special Force Operations
TM	Technical Manual
VFR	Visual Flight Rules
VNAF	South Vietnamese Air Force
VN	Viet Nam or Vietnam (US version)

NAMES AND PLACES

Many names of persons are real for their honor, credibility, and facts. Others are not real names to protect their identity and privacy. Any resemblance to persons living or dead resulting from similar names or identifying is entirely coincidental and unintentional.

The geographic locations are real, so are the facts and time frames related to the Viet Nam War and history as the best of the author's knowledge and recollection.

Chapter 1

THE WAR IS OVER

-oO*Oo-

"The war is over, sir."

At first, I strongly resisted. This could not be true. But then I saw the serious expression of the US Marines major, who stood only a couple of feet in front of me. He looked at me seriously; his lips closed tightly. Then he ordered me again, "Drop your weapon." Finally, I dropped my P38 pistol gun belt onto the floor deck of the USS *Okinawa* carrier with great disappointment in front of him.

The major seemed surprised that I didn't know what had happened. He ordered me to remove and surrender my aviation survival vest and knife. I complied and then requested an explanation. The major approached me, put his mouth against my ear, and said shortly and clearly, "The war is over, sir."

I raised both arms in the air with a gesture of total surprise and disappointment. The major and his two escort soldiers made a sharp and quick 180-degree turn, facing their backs to me. I understood that this was the proper protocol for a pilot landing an airplane in a foreign country. It was a part of the lesson I had learned from the US Armed Forces Instructor Pilot and the FAA Commercial Pilot training courses I had taken in 1972.

The interception escort brought me to the *Okinawa*'s lower deck. The major gave me a bottle of cold water, and his soldier handed me the US Immigration Application. I joined my wife and three little children, who were still in shock and seated in a dark corner of the cold metal bare floor.

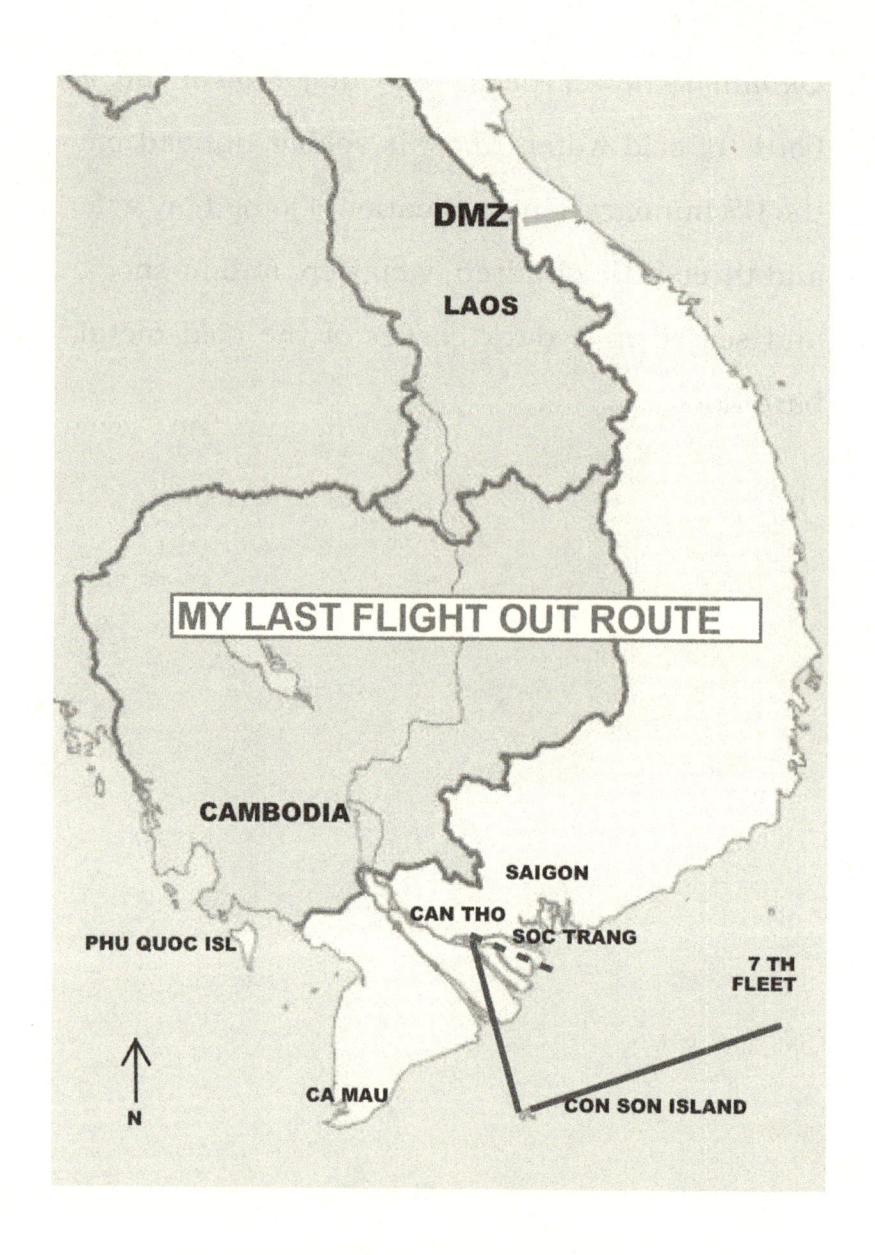

My Last Flight Out Flight Route

(Picture from the US Navy and AP)

They sat among the eighty passengers I had picked up, mostly the wives and children of the South Vietnamese Air Force officers who were left behind without husbands on Con Son Island in the last hours of utter hopelessness.

I could still hear the Marines Major saying, *"The war is over."* My eyes smarting with tears, I filled out the bilingual Immigration Application in Vietnamese and English.

I was in distress and devastation but had no idea what else I could do otherwise under this situation. I asked the major if I could go up to the deck. "What for?" he asked. I told him, "I would like to get my children's clothes from my luggage." The major glanced at me with a smile and made hand signals to follow him.

We walked up many sets of stairs to the carrier landing deck. It was cold and windy. A group of people with a small tractor were busy pushing my Chinook helicopter with "OOO" tail number off the deck and dumping it into the ocean. I couldn't believe what I was seeing and yelled out loud, "Why? Why did you dump my Chinook?" The major calmly replied, "To make room for more coming. To save lives, not aircraft." We both silently took many sets of stairs and walked back down below deck. No one said a word.

We were on the carrier ship on the high seas of the Pacific Ocean, which I believed was at least some 200 to 300 nautical miles from Vietnam territory. With sadness, horror, confusion, and terror, I realized that my nearly decade of military service to my country had ended. It was the darkest day of my life. I felt totally betrayed and helpless. I wasn't sure whom I should blame for the war and the loss of the war.

It was my longest day of flying without food, water, and sleep. It was the worst day of Vietnam history. It was the most terrible day of my life. It was the dark day of April 30, 1975, a day I will never forget.

Chapter 2

THE UNEXPECTED MISSION

-oO*Oo-

I received an order for the special mission from the base commander late in the evening of April 28, 1975, two days before my last flight out. The mission was to use four Chinooks to safely evacuate officers' wives and their children out of Can Tho Air Base to Con Son Island to avoid civilian casualties from the enemy shelling of the air base. The order also specified me, Major Con Nguyen, as the leader of this evacuation mission. Con Son Island is about 150 nautical miles south of Saigon.

The order was issued directly by the base commander, bypassing the War Room Operations, and sent directly to me. This order was very rare. It also stated that the take-off time would be given at the last minute and did not have details of any further actions after arriving and unloading the civilian passengers at the destination.

The order was an open-end without any further actions. Later, after I landed on the USS *Okinawa* carrier ship and received the immigration application to be accepted as a refugee, I understood that the order was a mission to escape with my family before the base commander and his high-level officers planned to leave the base for Thailand. It was a silent message to flee the country on the last day, which I did not realize at that time.

I didn't have time to go home to prepare for the trip. I asked my sergeant to return to my barracks to pick up my family in a big hurry without giving them enough details and time for packing adequate food and clothes.

I hardly found four flyable Chinooks. Only three Chinooks were equipped with landing lights. Besides, the entire squadron did not have any night flight training for years due to the restriction of fuel, spare parts, and allowable operation hours of each flyable aircraft per month. I took the aircraft without landing lights and gave the better ones to my wingmen.

My wife asked me where we were going. I explained to her and the other passengers that we were evacuating the air base tonight because the Viet Cong would attack the base. We waited in the long night for the final order from the base commander. I finally received the order *"clear to take-off"* at midnight from the base commander via FM radio channel around midnight.

We took off with four Chinooks fully loaded with civilians, including my wife and my three children in my Chinook. After about an hour flight, we finally landed on a small airstrip on Con Son Island very early on April 29. We didn't know what to do next, and no one believed we had abandoned the country to the communists.

I checked with the Con Son Airport control tower for the airport security and inquired the condition of the POL (Petroleum, Oil, and Lubrication) for refueling. An American airport traffic controller informed me that there was plenty of jet fuel at the airport. The only concern, he said, "Who and how to keep the airport in order, knowing every pilot would be fighting to refuel first when panic set in."

This American traffic controller warned me, "Although the airport Currently is secure; however, there are more than 10,000 communist prisoners in the military prison camps nearby." He also hinted, "These prisoners did not have any information from the outside or knew anything about the status of the war." He finally alerted me, "Otherwise, ... they would break out of jail and kill everybody on the island."

I decided to refuel the four Chinooks soon after landing and found a safe place to park. I carefully observed the condition and activities on the island, collected more information, and evaluated the situation. I called for a brief meeting with all the pilots on my team to discuss what we would do next to complete our assigned mission.

A couple of hours later, I cranked up the FM radio to contact the island airport tower. The American traffic controller at the airport had gone, and my communication was intercepted by a Vietnamese saying everything was under control and the island was safe and secure.

After discussion with the pilots on my team, I decided to leave behind one Chinook with my number two crew to support the passengers when needed. We took off with the three empty Chinooks to return to base, arriving at Con Tho Air Base about eight o'clock in the morning of April 29.

The area on the ground of Mekong Delta was unusually quiet, even some restricted areas where I flew over had previously encountered heavy enemy ground fire. It was obvious but questionable to me. I asked myself, "Where the Viet Cong moved its troops and antiaircraft machine guns to?" My instincts told me that some significant changes would soon be happening on the battlefield. Sure enough, after I landed at Can Tho home base, I received over UHF radio the order to surrender. The newly formed South Vietnamese government had unconditionally surrendered!

I got nervous, thinking about my family and others back on the island. I had to return to get them before it was too late.

I went to my office to double-check and verify the order. The new government was broadcasting over the radio station from Saigon, repeatedly ordering *"All soldiers must lay down your weapons... All pilots must return your aircraft to home base... All airports are closed... No airplanes are allowed to take off."*

This order was ridiculous. I went nuts. I refused to obey the order. No way in hell would I accept the surrender order from this newly formed government. I had to get out of here at any cost. I'd rather die than surrender to the communists. I thought deeply and decided to escape the base by any means.

During that night, I sneaked down to the aircraft parking area. I got the first available Chinook and one of my captain flight leaders, Captain Trong, took the second one. We took off without reporting to the air control tower. I received an order shortly after... "You must return to base immediately, or the two gunships heading to your way will shoot you down."

I told the pilots of the gunships do not get close to me because I would fly very fast at varying altitudes and had turned off all night lights, position lights and beacon light. Therefore, they would not be able to spot me out in the dark sky or to catch up to me. I also dared to collide with the gunships if they got near me. The two gunships did not know exactly where I was, so they could not chase me. I lost them.

It was a very dark night with heavy coastal thunderstorms on the ocean. We could not continue further out to the open sea, so we turned around and landed at Soc Trang Province. The local airport security police bused my ten crew members to the Soc Trang Province headquarters. A couple of minutes later, I was escorted by military police to see the province's chief.

The chief was very surprised when he saw me. I also recognized him right away as the former Special Operations officer of Ban Me Thuot base camp when I was a KingBee pilots' flight leader.

We looked at each other with a big question in our minds ...*What is happening?*

"Where are you heading to?" He asked suddenly.

"Out of here," I said.

"Then why you landed here?"

"Bad weather. It was a severe thunderstorm and very heavy rain on the ocean moving to the coastline."

"Where do you plan to go next?"

"Con Son Island."

"That is a big communist prisoner camp. It is very dangerous to be there."

"My family is there. I must pick them up then fly them to somewhere later."

"Did you see the Seventh Fleet or any rescue ships on the ocean?" He seriously asked me and was anxiously waiting for an answer.

"No. I did not see any. Why? Do you know something that I don't?" I questioned him and looked closely into his eyes for his true and honest answer.

"My wife and my children are now on the small boat heading out to the open sea with hope ... to be picked up by a rescue ship from the Seventh Fleet but I do not have any way to contact them..." He answered my question emotionally and nervously.

Someone knocked on his office door urgently. He left me alone and came back with a piece of paper in his hands and said, "This is the order from your air base headquarters that requested me to detain and send you and your men back to Can Tho Air Base."

I read the order, and I could not find the name or the title of the person who authorized to issue the order.

"Who issued this order?" I looked at him and asked.

"I do not know, Con. But... I have no alternative..." he said, then shook my hand and said, "Good luck, Major Con."

I thought this was the end of my escaping plan. My two Chinook crew members and I were in the bloody hands of the communists, who had already taken over the south. I opened my flight bag, pulled out my AR-15 with two pieces, a short barrel and a retractable stock, a very special assault weapon of the SOG team member. I assembled it to be ready to fire. I then sadly gave my AR-15 to him and said thoughtfully, "I wanted you to keep this. I have this weapon in my flight bag all the time when I fly. Now, it is yours."

He then asked me doubtfully, "Why you give to me?"

I responded to him sadly...that "Because...I do not want this weapon to fall into the hands of the enemy if they catch me."

Finally, my ten crew members were boarding a small helicopter as the passengers, and we had been escorted by two gunships to Can Tho home base at midnight on April 29th. I learned later that the Soc Trang Province was overrun by the communists a couple of hours after we left that night.

The military police escorted my two crew members to the airport security. After unloading from the military bus, ten of us were squeezed in a small room overnight. I kept listening to the air base security conversations over the hand-held two-way radio from the next-door office and recognized some big event was going on at the base.

I requested the guard to make a phone call to the base commander's office. His officer in charge said the general was not available. I placed another call to the general's residence. There was no answer there either. I felt something very wrong had happened. He had gone, perhaps!!! If there was no one in command of this air base, then who had ordered me to return to base and sent two gunships to escort me???

I hung up the phone and requested the security police sergeant to give me the details of the order to detain me along with my two crews. He responded politely, "You are not detained, sir. The door is unlocked." I got the message and told my crew members to get out of there quickly.

Early in the morning of the 30th, I hurried back to my squadron's headquarters to have a brief meeting with my pilots and crewmembers around nine o'clock.

Everyone was confused, worried, and frightened. Most of the pilots did not receive any directions and didn't know what to do and where to go. So, I told all the pilots and crew members of my squadron that "I'm no longer your commander." I made a very clear and urgent statement "It's time to escape and save your own and your families' lives."

There were many questions raised by my pilots. I told them to get out by any means. The government had surrendered. Some asked where we should go. I answered that we hoped to find the Seventh Fleet out on the ocean. They asked where the Seventh Fleet was. I told them I didn't know. One even asked which way I was going. I said... there were two options—south or southeast from here. I was going southeast since I left my family back there.

Before I left, I told them to exercise the survival skills individually—no one would lead anyone. I packed my flight bag with my helmet and survival vest and walked out of the squadron's office.

I crossed the taxiway and heard some gunfire in the airfield. Two mortars just landed and exploded in the nearby airport parking lot. There was a very loud noise of machine guns around the airport security fence. I ran across the runway to the Chinook parking.

The air base was out of order without any sign of enemy penetration. People ran from all directions looking for shelter. Gunfire continued all over the places.

I ran across the taxiway to get in the Chinook's parking lot. I grabbed the first one, started up the auxiliary power unit, and discovered it was low on fuel. I abandoned it and saw the next one with blades were turning, almost ready for taking off by one of my captains. I jumped in and put him in the co-pilot seat and taxied out. The tower was still giving traffic orders. When I was number two aircraft on the parallel taxiway, the first Chinook was taking off, but it got shot down after getting airborne, crashed and burned at the end of the runway.

I quickly changed the direction and made a very short, steep left turn on the top of the hangars. I escaped the gunfire. However, I still got hit by a small rifle. I flew at a low-level altitude to get out of the air base safely. Then quickly, I climbed up to 8,000 feet to avoid the enemy's antiaircraft machine guns from the restricted areas to the coastal.

After about fifteen to twenty minutes, I didn't see any signs of enemy activity on the ground, and there was no machine guns or rockets shooting up at me. So, I went down to a lower altitude, about 5,000 feet, and headed to the coastline.

As soon as I got over the ocean, the weather got worse. There were heavy showers and thunderstorms on the horizon, but I firmly believed it was more chance to survive on the high seas than in the mainland. I snaked through to the terrible rough weather, and finally, the Con Son Island was in sight.

I got to the end of the runway of Con Son Island in heavy rain showers. The airport was deserted. There was only a small group of civilians, including my wife and children. I picked them up and parked at the air terminal.

About an hour after, there were many helicopters and small airplanes that landed after they completed their daily missions. In a couple of hours later, the airfield was full of airplanes and helicopters. Everyone wanted to cut in line to refuel first.

I saw the problem worsen, thinking that people would kill each other for refueling. I took my two gunmen as my escorts and declared to all pilots that I'm now the commander of this airfield. Everyone should obey my orders, or I would have them shot and killed right on the spot.

The pilots followed my order to line up to refuel. At the time I went to refuel my Chinook, all the passengers resisted leaving my aircraft. I had to get out of the pilot's seat and walked behind my Chinook with my passengers to prove to them that I would not take off without them after we refueled.

I gave orders to all the airmen and soldiers to pick up their weapons and all ammunition to defend ourselves. I needed to figure out what to do and where to go next. It was about 2:30 to 3:00 p.m. when I sent one Huey to scout out the ocean for any signs of ships from the Seventh Fleet. About an hour later, he made a forced landing on the sand bar because he ran out of fuel.

I pulled him out from his crippled helicopter and saved him. Most people didn't bother to ask him how he was doing but wanted to know right away if he saw any ships out on the ocean. He replied that he saw some far away but had no radio contact.

At about 4:00 p.m., a couple of Chinooks from my squadron came out and landed. I got the helicopter pilots together and told them that there were two options. We could find one small island to land on, defend ourselves for one night, and hope that someone could rescue us the next morning, knowing that there were 10,000 communist prisoners on the island that could break out of prisons at any time. Or, we could take the risk of flying out immediately and hope that we could find the Seventh Fleet on the open sea.

Many pilots took off and went in many different directions. I came back to my Chinook and still saw the same number of passengers sitting tied on the cargo floor. I asked them to leave, but they resisted. They asked me, "Major, where are you going now?" I replied to them, "I have one way out, and hopefully, I will find the Seventh Fleet ... somewhere out on the Pacific Ocean."

One young woman asked me, "What would happen if you didn't find the Seventh Fleet?" I replied to her, "I would not return, and I would ditch the Chinook in the ocean with my family and die together ... that's why I've asked all of you to leave my helicopter." I heard many voices from many female passengers saying they would die with me. Four, five soldiers quickly picked up their rifles and walked off my aircraft.

Finally, I took off my lucky "OOO" tail number Chinook, headed out to the sea at around four p.m. I maintained 8,000 feet with minimum power settings to hopefully extend the flight time longer, just in case we found no place to land.

The ocean was so vast. The horizon was dark gray. We felt so little and lost in the giant gloomy skies and mysterious ocean. All radio communications were deadly silent. It was very scary, very fearful, and very intense under the unbreakable silence that I never experienced. I wondered if there was anybody out there on the high seas to provide any hope for this crew, helpless women, and small children.

While I maintained the control, everyone looked out in all directions with the hope of sighting the Seventh Fleet anywhere on the horizon.

About thirty minutes of flying, we saw nothing and heard nothing. Then I decided to reduce the altitude to 6,000 feet. Nothing changed, but the ocean became choppy. I continued to fly, heading ninety degrees and maintaining the same speed. Then I asked my crewmembers to look out and down for any signs of a boat, ship, or any object on the water. They all said, "Negative." There was nothing in sight.

After about an hour flight, I spotted a big ship on the horizon at exactly twelve o'clock in my direction. I tried to make emergency radio contact, but there was no response.

I stared at the horizon and kept flying. Then I climbed back to 8,000 feet, and the ship disappeared. I thought that I saw a mirage of the ship instead. Then I decided to go back down to 6,000 feet. The ship then reappeared on the horizon. This time I asked my co-pilot, "Do you see the ship at twelve o'clock?" He said, "Affirmative, there's a ship at twelve o'clock."

I climbed back up again and saw nothing, no ship on the horizon. This time I asked my co-pilot if he saw the ship. He responded, "Negative" again.

I was nervous, really nervous! I could feel my sweat running down on my back and my cold blood raced down under my skin. I changed the heading a bit, by five, ten degrees or so, and then descended to 6,000 feet. That ship reappeared on the horizon. I asked my co-pilot to confirm the ship on the horizon. He replied, "Positive."

I changed the heading to different directions, about twenty degrees left and right. I asked my flight engineer and the loadmaster at both side of the aircraft the same question. Both confirmed there was a ship on the horizon.

I returned to my original course and flew straight to the direction of the ship. About fifteen to twenty minutes later, instead of seeing the big ship on the horizon, I spotted a smaller gray ship in sight at long distance. My co-pilot confirmed the same. I descended to 2,000 feet above the water. We both maintained the ship in our sights.

We discovered the ship had no flag but was armed with four big-barrel machine guns aimed at us. As soon as we flew closer to it, the barrels turned to and followed us. On the radio emergency channel, it was silent. No one was contacting us.

I decided to fly back up to 6,000 feet and keep the original course. Five to ten minutes later, I saw more and bigger ships occupying a large area of water on the ocean. I also knew all ships were traveled in a formation, at the same speed, same position, and same direction, with white water trails in the back and black smokestacks in the air. Far on the horizon and in the center of the ship formation, there was a giant black ship, traveling the same speed without a smokestack in the air. I quickly thought that it must be the USS *Enterprise* atomic-powered aircraft carrier.

I headed straight to the biggest ship, the *Enterprise*. Suddenly I received radio contact on my VHF emergency channel. It requested that "The aircraft heading ninety degrees east to identify yourself and report your altitude." I replied, "This is VNAF (Vietnamese Air Force) Chinook Triple Zero, 6,000 feet, heading ninety degrees east." It requested me to change to a working frequency, and I complied.

During the conversation, the USS *Enterprise* aircraft carrier gave a series of commands for me to change my altitude and heading several times. I followed the orders and figured out that my final heading was just about thirty degrees off from my original heading to the Enterprise. At the same time, it asked where I learned to fly a Chinook. I responded back, "Fort Rucker, Alabama." It asked for my class number. I replied, "1972". It asked if I remembered the instructor pilot. I gave the name. It asked if I had any friends who are American. I gave the names "Carl Nelson, Brian Scott, Bob Morris."

The final important communication was this message: "There will be a giant orange flag that will appear quickly on the horizon, at your thirty degrees heading. That is where you will be landing."

I turned the aircraft to the left, heading to thirty degrees. I told my co-pilot to keep his eyes closely on the horizon. Suddenly, an orange panel raised up and folded down quickly on the ship. Then I continued to fly and changed to a different radio working frequency to contact the ship as it requested.

I recognized this carrier ship was much bigger than the other ships nearby and had a very short runway. Later, I realized it was the USS *Okinawa* aircraft carrier.

When I got closer to the carrier ship, the order was given: "You have one chance to land. No go-around."

I saw the gun barrels pointed to me. I replied, "Roger, no go-around."

I descended to 500 feet above the water. The order was repeated, "You have only one chance to land. No go-around."

I replied again, "Roger that," and reported that I was at the downwind and ready to land.

When I was at the final approach, I saw a couple of small Cessna airplanes missed the runway, hooking their front landing wheels on the ship deck rail and burning. Many helicopters fell short on the final approach, missed the landing deck, and went into the water.

Nobody rescued anyone. Those indications told me that the ships were moving forward at a very fast speed, about ten to fifteen knots or more, easily. I quickly decided that I would land with forwarding speed at least twenty miles per hour at touch-down with forward speed to catch up to this moving landing deck.

The runway was very short. In front of the runway was the control tower. If I hit it, I would crash and burn, and there was no chance to go around. I touched down with forwarding speed as planned.

I hit and held down the brakes firmly and killed the engines instantly. Everyone was safe. I was stunned, remaining in my seat, and not able to do anything.

Meanwhile, the passengers got out of the Chinook. The rotor blades were still turning. My co-pilot completed the shutdown procedure and got out.

I took off my helmet and hooked it up on the cockpit ceiling. I saw three Marines, two soldiers and one major, waiting for me on the deck. I slowly got out of the Chinook, and they intercepted me right away. It occurred to me that my new life had started and that... *the war was over.*

Chapter 3

MIRACLE AND FAITH

-oO*Oo-

It was my two longest days, from the midnight of April 28, 1975, to the last minute when I landed on the USS *Okinawa* carrier, April 30, 1975, I had no food, little water, and no sleep. However, my spirit was well uplifted and very strong determinative. My mind was remaining sharp, clear, and calm. I had made many critical decisions within a slip of the second, without having any information, without knowing what was happening to my country.

I made the decision to return to Can Tho home base and take care of people in my squadron in the last minutes, the decision to leave my family on Con Son Island, the decision to disobey the government surrender order, the decision to come back to pick up my family, along with many helpless ladies and children who were left behind on the island overnight, the decision to head out to the high seas without knowing where to land. Those decisions have changed my family's and my lives forever.

After I took off from Con Son Island and returned to Can Tho Air Base, there were several C130s from Bien Hoa Air Base, north of Saigon, that fled Vietnam very earlier morning of April 30. They stopped on the island to pick up only families whose husbands were with them and then headed to U-Tapao, Thailand. Since I was not there, C130 pilots did not allow my wife and my children to boarding the planes.

After the C130s had gone, so had the last hope of the people who stuck behind on the island. My wife had only one last option to escape by carrying our three kids to board a small merchant ship docked a distance from the shore. Linda held my youngest one while the two other ones ran alongside, from the airport to shore. They were exhausted from the sand, sun, and heat.

Luckily, Linda found the keys to a military Jeep abandoned at the end of the runway. She loaded the children in and drove toward the beach. The ship was visible from the airport, so Linda kept driving toward the ocean. The gravel road then turned to the dirt tracks and finally, it ended about halfway to the ship. Linda and the children had to walk a far distance across the rocky hills, heavy bushes, and many sand dunes to the shore.

Our middle child lost her shoes, so her feet were badly burned. The boat was docked far from the shore in the deep water. My wife could not make it, and the kids almost drowned, so she decided to go back to the island airport terminal. That decision had brought my family and me together to make the next venture for my last flight out. It was a miracle. I believed that good faith kept us alive and reunited during that day.

Linda and I have faith in Buddha. Others believe in God. No one believes those decisions could be made by a human alone in those situations. As a combat pilot, I carried a picture of Buddha Quan Am in my flight bag at all times. I still have the picture with me now, the only valuable item I had with me when I came to the US. Quan Am helped us to keep our mind clear so we could have made a series of very crucial life or death decisions in a very short time and without having any facts or information.

In looking back from the evacuation mission in the midnight hour of the 28th to the moment I landed on the USS *Okinawa* carrier very late on April 30th, 1975, I did not believe I had made those decisions by myself. My good faith in my Quan Am had played a significant role in helping me to overcome such extreme adversity.

(Picture of Quan Am)

Chapter 4

JOURNEY ON THE HIGH SEAS

-oO*Oo-

The Seventh Fleet continued its mission to rescue the pilots who could escape out of Viet Nam the day after the surrender and started to sail out to the international waters of the Pacific Ocean. Therefore, all civilians must be unloaded out of the carrier of the naval fleet as soon as possible.

The Marines loaded all the refugees in the landing crafts waiting on the bottom of the *Okinawa* aircraft carrier. These were big rectangular flat-bottom metal boats with a big ramp open in the front and the engine in the back, designed to launch troops quickly to shore. We were all sitting inside the landing crafts, waiting to be transferred to an unknown place. Everyone sat down flat on the bottom of the craft and were worried that we didn't know how our next journey on high seas would be.

After a couple of hours waiting in the dark, the landing crafts left the *Okinawa* carrier late at night and headed out to the high seas.

The choppy waves were so rough, and the landing crafts were too small, like many dead leaves jumping up and down from one wave to another. It did not take long for everyone to be nervous and get seasick. We didn't realize where we were going, and no one told us anything. All I knew for sure was that the refugees had to get off the USS *Okinawa* carrier after signing the immigration application form given by the US Marines.

After almost a long hour in the darkness of the open seas, we found ourselves outside a big, tall merchant ship. The landing craft shone its headlights at the ship's hull. I couldn't believe we were expected to board that merchant ship from the outside of the ship at night in the middle of the Pacific Ocean.

There was an outwardly inclined, curvy, narrow, twisted ladder covered by very slippery green algae with no signs of use ever. It was an emergency maintenance ladder outside of the ship. Our landing crafts jumped up and down crazily next to the big merchant ship, which seemed more stable on the deep water.

The Merchant Ship

We were on the water about fifty to sixty feet below the merchant ship's deck. The metal hull was corroded, rough, and dangerous. I saw an old lady already passed out from just looking at the ladder on the big ship. The ladder had many rungs and looked very slippery and very scary.

At least five or six US Marines already on the deck of the ship, extending their arms out to catch those who reached the top of the deck before losing their grip or falling off from exhaustion.

But not all the climbers made it. I saw some just dropped off the landing craft and sink into the water while trying to grab the first ladder rung. Others fell off the ladder at the beginning of the inverted curve of the ladder that followed the shape of the ship's hull. You could only hold on to the ladder by your hands, while your feet and body were dangling in the air. The wind was strong enough to blow your body off the ladder and throw you into the rough and cold waters.

There was no time to spare, and no one bothered to rescue anyone. It was the game of our ultimate survival. There was nothing that I learned and practiced on the Sea Survival lesson in the flight school, which I could compare to this experience. The real experience of life or death.

There was a flood of light from the top of the ship that was shining down the ladder to indicate the ladder we had to climb up to board the ship. The narrow and long ladder was straight up and curved outward along with the shape of the hull. The rusty ladder inclined reversely wrapped around the curvy body of the ship. Therefore, the floodlights from the deck missed many rungs of the lower part of the emergency ladder where we needed to see most. I saw people were trying very hard to grab the ladder with the waves raising it up and down. Some missed the first rung, dropped into the sea and disappeared.

However, if we sat in the landing craft any longer, we'd be exhausted, dizzy and nauseous. I felt there was no way better than to get on board the merchant ship as soon as possible. We had to board the ship, unprepared and quickly. We had no choice.

I decided to hold my son and passed my middle child to Sergeant Song, my flight engineer. I gave the youngest daughter to my wife, Linda. I boarded first. My four-year-old son was so scared when I climbed up higher. He held my neck so tight that I thought I would be choked to death.

I used my last energy to grab one rung at a time without looking down at the water. I couldn't believe that I got aboard the merchant ship. There was no assistance, no one looking out for another. I sat my boy on the steel deck and looked down, hoping that my sergeant would be able to carry my older daughter up. Since he was younger and stronger than me, trying his best, he made it on board.

My biggest concern was Linda and my youngest child. I knew it would require a miracle, but she got up finally with my little baby wrapped around her chest. It was a miracle that she made it. We all climbed down the inside vertical stairs to go to the bottom hull of the ship. This was a cargo ship for transporting goods, not humans. Therefore, there was no insulation, no heating, no toilets, and no drinking water.

Everyone sat next to each other on the bare metal floor like sardines in a fish can. It did not take long for body heat to make the air hot, stuffy, and stinking from human odor. Some passengers passed out after a while. I looked up around the deck. There was at least one platoon of Marines with loaded rifles walking around, keeping an eye on the refugees to make sure everyone was following the orders.

In the early morning, I realized that there were around a couple thousand refugees stacked in the bottom floor of this merchant ship. I heard some gunfire on the deck. I was told the Marines were shooting any violent people after their warning failed to keep the crowd in order and save the lives of the rest. Because the merchant ship was overcrowded, the sun was baking; the human odor was getting heavy. Several people passed out and died. I stood up and walked around to get more information. I was told that the ship would sail to Guam soon.

Everybody was starving and thirsty, but the merchant ship was not equipped with any accommodation for food or water to support this big crowd picked up from the sea.

The Marines threw sliced bread out for people. Most were broken apart, and people picked up crumbs from the floor to eat for survival. Soon, they ran out of bread. The Marines then used thirty-gallon galvanized trash cans to cook rice soup with tuna fish, stirring it with a regular metal shovel. The ship stayed still, so the air was hard to breathe. More people passed out from the lack of oxygen and fresh air.

The Marines didn't know how to feed these people without any plates, bowls, or containers. They used the shovel to pour the soup as people held two hands together to hold the soup. Most of the soup spilled on the floor.

I was afraid my children would die because I could not get soup or water for them. When the Marines prepared the next meal for the day, I walked in and asked if I could be a helper. I helped them cook the soup by pouring the rice out of the bag and into the boiling water in the thirty-gallon trash can. Ten to thirty minutes later, the Marines opened a couple of one-gallon tuna fish cans. I volunteered to pour the tuna cans into the hot soup for them. After emptying the cans, I kept one for myself.

When the soup started to cool off, the Marines would repeat the same thing, using the shovel to stir the soup and pouring it into the hands of people. I then used my empty can to receive the soup for five members of my family without having to use my two hands to make a bowl. That empty can of tuna fish have saved my children from starvation and dehydration. I protected that empty tuna fish can like it was the most important item in my life. Later, other people used hats, shoes, scarves, clothes, or any other object to hold the soup and bring it to their children or for themselves.

The second day of the journey on the high seas was even tougher because of the lack of fresh air in the bottom floor of the merchant ship. Therefore, many people passed out and died on the bottom floor of the ship. Since there were no toilets or sanitization available, I could smell human waste all over the place. I had to figure out how to save my family's lives.

I wandered to the upper deck. It was frigid and windy. However, there was plenty of fresh air to keep the human alive. The ship carried heavy construction equipment and merchandise containers that were stacked up vertically. I discovered a huge cardboard box under a big, new, yellow bulldozer. I opened it and saw some attachments, spare parts, manuals, and instruction papers. I moved those spare parts out of the box to make enough room for the five of us to crawl into the empty cardboard box under the bulldozer. I would use the box as a shelter to keep my family alive.

I went down to the bottom floor to figure out how to carry up each member of my family, once at a time, to stay in the empty box. The stairs from the lower hull to the upper deck were high and vertical with round metal bar rungs, but it was better than the maintenance ladder outside of the merchant ship. Slowly and surely, I moved each member of my family to the upper deck, so that we could get fresh air and keep ourselves together and alive.

We crawled all together inside the box to keep our body heat and protect the children from hypothermia. We stayed the whole night and felt better, even in the freezing cold weather. At mealtime, I continued to help the soldiers to prepare the rice soup again. I used the empty tuna can to get a full can of soup. I carried it up to feed my family and kept them fed and warm.

More people were dying on the third day. I saw the Marines dump the dead bodies into the water and kept going on in the journey. I didn't know exactly how many people died. For that reason, the ship then changed its destination. Instead of going straight to Guam, the ship stopped by Subic Bay in the Philippines. That change had reduced more deaths, and everyone was so happy.

Feet on The Ground Again

On the fourth day, we got off the ship and moved to a picnic area on the US air base. To this day, I still remember clearly the wonderful taste of fresh orange and hard-boiled eggs that were laid around the coconut trees. We grouped and rested together; we knew we had made it alive. The fresh food, water, oranges, and hard-boiled eggs had saved our lives. That taste has been imprinted into my brain, and even now, I've never found anything that tasted better than that.

The Marines then assembled some military tents and cots so that we could lay down and rest for a day or two in the picnic area of the base. When I stayed there, there were a couple of civilians who came to visit the refugee camp. There was one person who looked at my military hat. He mentioned that he really liked my hat. I told him that I could sell it to him as a souvenir. He gave me two dollars. I used those first two dollars I made in my survival journey to buy food and drinks for a couple of days for my family in the first camp.

The next day, the workers of the camp gave me a set of old civilian clothes and told me I couldn't wear my South Vietnamese Air Force military uniform in the Philippines air base because of the political situation. I changed to the used civilian clothes and felt I was now totally and voluntarily discharged from my Vietnamese Air Force.

A couple of days later, US Air Force transported the refugees out of Subic Bay and to Guam by C141, under pressure from the Communist Party of the Vietnamese government. My life was dramatically changed, and suddenly I lost everything, my country, my home, my military career after almost ten years in service, and obviously, I became an immigrant. However, I was still happy because I had my family with me. So, my children would not be repeating my terrible childhood or facing a horrible war.

Chapter 5

A LONELY CHILD

-oO*Oo-

I was born in 1941 after my father died, my mother said. No one knew why my father died, even my mother. Back then, men could have more than one wife and as many children as they wanted. Since my mother was the second wife, I grew up outside of the primary family circle, on my mother's side. We were considered secondary relatives from my father in terms of the family blood relationship. Therefore, no one outside of my direct family really cared for me, no tight blood relationship, and no family property that I inherited. My childhood was lonely, and my family was destitute.

My mother told me she did not have enough rice to cook soup to feed me when I was a baby. Everyone was starving, and we did not have enough food or warm clothes in the winter. That was the time the Japanese bombed the Viet Nam only north-south railroad and the Highway One running parallel to it. It was during the middle of WWII. The Japanese defeated the French colonies in Viet Nam. Within a very short period, all southeast Asia was under control of the Empire of the Rising Sun.

A half-million Vietnamese died by starvation. I was a lucky one, surviving as a baby. The southern part of Viet Nam had a lot of rice surplus but could not do anything with it except to burn it like charcoal for fuel while the center of Viet Nam had nothing to eat and the northern part of Viet Nam was suffering from the lack of food supplies. The War had expanded from cities to the countryside. Death, sickness, and starvation were spreading everywhere.

Viet Nam was a part of the WWII southeast Asian battlefield. Hai Lang was my district of the northern part of Quang Tri Province, the most unfortunate part of Viet Nam. This region is the part of the flatlands built up with sand and mud carving down from the high mountains. This long and narrow flatland was a giant gutter collecting rainwater off the Truong Son Mountain chain on the west and dumping it into the Pacific Ocean on the east. Sand dunes, streams, creeks, ponds, muddy lakes, and rice paddies made up the transition of the high elevation from the mountains to the sea.

In the rainy season, called *monsoon*, the rainwater collected from the mountainsides, rushed into the short and narrow rivers and created severe flooding over the entire region for months. And in the long summers, hot winds blowing from Laos carried extreme heat and dry air, turning ponds, lakes, rivers, and rice paddies into hard clay and wiping out all the water-living species.

There were not many resources I knew of in this area except lumber in the jungle and fish in the sea. However, Viet Nam was an underdevelopment country then, so there was no modern technology or heavy equipment to leverage these resources. Most people living in my village had very hard lives. They labored for the very little hope of making enough food to feed themselves and their family. They grew rice, potatoes, and veggies to eat, but never knew whether they would have a chance to harvest them before floods, hurricanes, and other natural disasters might take all away. They had tough lives but stuck with the land where they were born, lived, and died.

The Japanese surrendered in 1945, at the end of WWII. Then the French returned to Indochina to re-establish its colonial states with financial and military support from the United States of America. The communists then regrouped and started the new French Resistance War. I grew up in this different war with plenty of violence, death, and destruction.

In the middle of 1954, the French surrendered to the Vietnamese communists and left Viet Nam. At that time, I had just turned twelve years old. My older brother was forced by the communists to carry supplies and ammunition for them to the jungle. He died just a year before the French were defeated and left Indochina. My sisters married men from both sides and rarely saw each other.

The DMZ

The superpower nations then decided to divide my little country into two parts, North and South Vietnam, separated by a DMZ (Demilitarized Zone) of five kilometers width on each side along the Ben Hai River within the Seventeenth Latitude. The DMZ was a deep scar imaginary line, located at the northern province of Quang Tri.

The North called themselves the "Democratic Republic of Viet Nam" and the South was the "Republic of Viet Nam". Both names sounded alike, so were the same people living in the two countries. However, they turned themselves into enemies to kill each other with the foreign forces behind them.

By the Geneva Accords 1954, both sides were not allowed to have any weapons within the DMZ. Although it was only true in theory, the North

Vietnamese troops were heavily armed, crossing the river and along the Ho Chi Minh trails to South Vietnam at nights.

The Hien Luong Bridge connecting the North and the South and crossed the Ben Hai River, but no one dared to walk on it unless you wanted to be shot by soldiers from both sides.

This division was deeply embedded not only geographically, but also culturally and mentally into the people from the North and South.

(Quang Tri Province Map and the DMZ)

They thought differently, believed in different ways, lived different lives, and died at different places. The North brainwashed its young people proudly to be born from the North, to go south to die for the country to liberate the South Vietnamese from the American imperialists and capitalists. The South promoted the new generation to arm and to kill the North Vietnamese for freedom.

This time, Americans were directly involved with tightly controlling the South Vietnamese government to engage my poor country into the game of death with the Chinese communists dominating North Vietnam.

After the ceasefire from the Geneva Accords of 1954, I walked with my mother for a whole day, crossing many small villages, mud ponds, sand dunes, creeks, and rice paddies in the countryside to make my first homecoming to my father's village. The village had been in the combat zone just directly south of the DMZ. I did not see any men or even male teens. All I saw were older women, children, dogs, cats, and chickens who were living in grass huts or bomb shelters. Their homes were destroyed to the ground with barely a trace of footings and foundation left.

No one from the foreign countries took the time to allow the Vietnamese babies and children to grow up quickly enough to supply the human force needed for the new war that they wanted, planned, and that we had to fight for!!!

South Vietnam was a vital American checkpoint in its Pacific Rim Strategy to isolate and control the Red China expansion. The Chinese supplied North Vietnam with food and plenty of weapons and committed *fighting the American capitalists to the last Vietnamese soldier!* The new battle began on a much larger scale.

I was born in one war, grew up during a different war, and fought the new war to the end. I fought the war we did not start, and I finished the war we did not end. This war was horrible. This war was just a showdown of the foreign forces with the modern weapons from the outside superpowers. This war created a terrible killing field with the most senseless destruction to my little country, Viet Nam.

My Quang Tri Province

Because of the Viet Nam war, many places became well known in my poor little province of Quang Tri, where many big battles took place. Khe Sanh, Con Thien, and Lang Vei were the places for the games of death. These meat grinders left numerous dead bodies strewn across the battlefields without any justifiable objectives. The soil in those areas was deeply soaked with human blood from all sides. These places had been chosen for the bloody stages of the stupid games of death: **to kill or just be killed**.

Both sides geared up with all foreign modern weapons: new and just modified airplanes, bombers, helicopters, gunships, armed AC130, F4C Phantom jet fighters, B52, Cobra attack helicopters, new helicopter gunships, new tanks, new SAM missiles, new rockets, new antiaircraft machine guns, new mobile artilleries, modern rifles, new hand grenades, etc., to test each other in proving who could kill more and who could kill other side quickly and instantly.

The North even used the old-fashioned Chinese tactic of mass-human-waves attack against bullets from machine guns, new grenade launchers, new mortars, modified AR-15 rifles, etc. Both sides came in with the most powerful forces to kill or to be killed. They wiped out anything moving. They destroyed everything above the surface of the earth. After the brutal match, both sides picked up their dead bodies and declared their own victory and silently withdrew from the blood-bathed battlefields like Khe Sanh68, Khe Sanh71, Lang Vei, Con Thien, Hamburger Hill, A Shau Valley, Duc Co, Dak To, Dak Lak, Loc Ninh, etc.

Both sides further learned that killing was just a simple way of eliminating the enemy in the battlefields, but it did not cause serious suffering or effectively terrify the remaining. The communists created the booby traps with bamboo or metal sharp sticks pointing upward and the other end planted firmly into the bottom of a well dug up deep hole covered with a thin layer of dirt or grass. With a small mistake, a soldier would fall into the trap with a number of those sharp bamboo or metal sticks piercing through the feet. The unfortunate victim would be stuck painfully in the deep hole with his feet locked in an immobile position until death and among the presence of helpless comrades. This cruel weapon really scared the hell out of the soldiers and took down their will to fight as well.

The Americans discovered a better way to wound more Viet Cong than just to kill them. They were discovering the nail rockets, which spread out hundreds of sharp pins from the air and flew into the enemy's body to keep them immobile but still alive. When one got wounded by those pins, it would take three or four others to take care of their painfully wounded buddy. The entire unit faced death-in-the water, stuck in the same position for a long time.

More suffering would cause less effectiveness to the enemy's mobility and morale in the battlefield than just killing to eliminate them. How much sinning could humans do to each other? But it had done widely in the Vietnam War. Believe it or not.

Chapter 6

POOR FAMILY

-oO*Oo-

I started to realize after I finished elementary school that there were many places in Vietnam where there was land that promised a better life than my hometown. The life in my mother's village was not in my future, but I had to finish high school first before moving to the south to begin my quest. My problem was that I did not have any money or anyone who could help me get started.

Fortunately, I had my elementary school principal who had shown an interest in my advancing education. He asked me if I had registered for the screening test to qualify for high school in the coming year. I was his best student with the highest score of the entire Quang Tri Province. He was concerned for me and wanted to see me continue my education. I told the principal that my family could not afford for me to go to high school due to the cost of living away from home. He told me that I could ride a bicycle to school, twelve kilometers one way. I responded that I did not have a bike. He tapped my shoulder and encouraged me to take the test first. So, I did.

I rode the bus with my friend from my village to Quang Tri City, but we didn't know where to stay for the three days of the selection examination.

We decided to walk, crossing town to the other edge of the city with the hope that we could stay in the pagoda. We explained our situation and asked the monk for permission to stay for a couple of nights. There was a significant relief when the monk said, "Your boys can stay in the corner of the floor of the public worship area. There is no food available but water is in the well in the backyard."

We gathered any dimes we had to buy a couple of loaves of bread and noodles and walked across town during those three days. The monk was delighted to see that we swept and cleaned the pagoda floor. We thanked him before we left.

The principal was following up with the students who passed the examination. He saw my name in the final qualifications list. He told me I passed the test and asked me if my parents had prepared me to start school in a couple of days. I told him that my mom did not have any money to support my high school. He understood and told me that he would allow me to stay with his family. He would give me a ride on the back of his scooter to the city.

That was the happiest day for me, knowing I would go to Nguyen Hoang, the province high school. I kept my grades up every day and showed him my quarterly report cards in appreciation for the chance to continue my education. The principal was very proud of me and was pleased to help.

I moved in with his relative's family the second year with a part-time job tutoring a ten-year-old kid while I finished high school. With the government scholarship in the years following, I had some money for my books and my first bicycle. My high school principal also allowed me to have one classroom in the school for my private summer school to help other students get ready for the next school year. I continued tutoring and moved from one family to the next during my college years at Hue City, which was far away from my hometown.

The Vietnam War expanded in magnitude. Terrorists, bombings, assassinations, and killings took place every day, anywhere in the city. Hue was no longer an old traditional and peaceful city. Demonstrations, protesting, and kidnapping made the city very unstable, politically and economically. The communists gained the most control in the countryside and were approaching the edges of most cities. Many areas in South Vietnam were under the dual control of the South government during the day and the communists at night.

Chapter 7

NATIONAL MILITARY ACADEMY DA LAT

-oO*Oo-

Because I was the last male in my family, I was excused from the military draft. However, I felt I would be more vulnerable to be uninvolved or to remain in the middle of the military conflict without a piece of metal in my hands to protect myself in a country fully loaded with all kinds of weapons and conflicts. I could be killed by either side. So, I had no choice but to get involved and play an unwanted game with a better position and better training. I volunteered to join the National Military Academy at Da Lat.

The total number of cadets selected in my class was around 250. I was in the "A" company, the first of eight companies of the cadet battalion including the senior class cadets.

The first sixty days were very rough. There were a lot of physical demands that I never believed my body could handle. However, this routine was repeatedly enforced daily, so I pushed myself above the limit and my body, and my mind kept advancing to the next target level and moving on to the harder one. I felt all the muscles in every part of my body tired and exhausted. I needed to rest, but I never had a chance to do so. Food and sleeping became the biggest demands of the body.

My difficulty in sleeping habits when I was in college just suddenly disappeared. I could sleep any time now, in a couple of minutes or a whole night long. It did not matter. Noise, light, in the bed or on the floor, in the classroom, standing up, sitting down, or even walking, did not stop me from sleeping. I stood straight in my attention position with my rifle on my shoulder and looked at the officer face and slept with my eyes wide open while he was giving his lectures.

There were only three meals a day with stringent rules; sitting up square and straight on only a half front seat with the back straight up parallel with the back of the chair but, unlike the senior cadets, do not dare to lean back onto the back of the chair. Fork and spoon must be on the plate and hands must be rested on the thighs before you can chew food in your mouth. All those procedures slowed you down to consume the meal; however, there were only thirty minutes to finish the meal. So, eat fast or be starving later.

There was no resting time, even a minute, after the meals, and we were forced to run and resumed other activities scheduled for the day. During the first several days, my stomach was upset, my abdomen could not tolerate it, and I could not follow the order. Several other classmates had the same problems. The senior cadet drill team then forced us to do more push-ups, more jumping, and fast running. Magically, my body found a way to change and adapt to a tougher situation. I survived and moved on to the next obstacle with harsher physical punishment.

Seven days a week, twenty-four hours a day, I was under the command of the senior cadets. Push-ups, jumping, running, climbing—there were very few lucky minutes that I could be allowed to march. The basic training made everyone look tougher and stronger.

The High Mountain Peak

After eight weeks of hard physical training without any break, here came the class's big day. The day to conquer the Lam Vien Mountain Peak before being accepted as new cadets of the Military Academy.

Lam Vien is the highest peak of the mountain on the west side of Da Lat City. Our journey took a day by trucks to the foothill of the mountain, overnighted with military tactical guards and defense practices to exercise what we had learned in the past two months.

It was cold and windy, and we were told this was the usual climate on this higher elevation. We all had taken turns playing night guard two hours at night and packed up early the next morning. We lined up ready to run up the white cloud-covered mountain peak with twenty-five-pound backpacks and M1 rifles on hands in ready-to-fire position.

It was a beautiful jungle with many wildflowers, birds, and animals, but I did not have time to enjoy those. Everyone kept running to the point of almost vertical incline, then we were slowed down at the narrow path and took turns climbing up step by step with our rifles on our backs to free our hands to grab the sharp stuck-out rocks and tree branches, in order to pass this challenging section.

We were totally exhausted at the halfway point with several steeper climbing sections remaining. The sky started to clear out, and the white-cloud-cap moved away. It was beautiful and very picturesque. We pushed ourselves forward, and the senior cadet drill teams tried to slow our advancing by ambushing at every sharp turn and tight corners. They even shot at us with blank bullets and threw out the training hand grenades to terrify us.

My "A" company reached the Lam Vien high mountain peak first. Everyone stood up straight and yelled very loud to mark our accomplishment. We could see clearly the entire area from there to the Pacific Ocean. However, our time of celebration was too short. The "C" company just got up to our standing ground. They forced my "A" company down and took the spot and claimed it was time for their victory.

A day after our return to the academy, the Class 21 members, who made it through our first two months of physical training, were accepted as new cadets. We earned the Red Alpha insignia in a big traditional military ceremony. The first stage of training had turned us from college students to soldiers. The next stage waiting for cadets would be harder to transform a cadet to a military officer, a lieutenant, who should be ready for the battlefields.

The Cadet Hierarchy

There was a hierarchy in our Cadet Battalion where the seniors enjoyed most of their privileges. They walked on the center hallways where the new cadets must clean daily but were not supposed to use. They ate at different times in the mess hall with longer periods and more relaxing environment. The seniors enjoyed family visiting more often during the weekends while the new cadets had limited time and were mostly busy during the weekends.

I did not have any family members visiting, unlike my roommate Bau, whose family was in Saigon. He told me the first time visiting, his mother looked at him from head to toes and cried very hard. He felt very embarrassed, but he could not stop her from crying. His mother kept hold of his hands and looked at his ten big fingers with huge dark knuckles and asked, "What have they been doing to you?" Then she touched his face with dark and rough skin and cried again.

Bau kept telling his mom that he was fine, stronger, and could handle the change. He asked his mom not to worry about him, and there was nothing wrong at all. His mom promised to revisit him next weekend, but Bau was on duty, so she was very sad. Bau kept telling her, "This is the military academy, not a college. Sorry, Mom."

Da Lat is a small city on the central highlands of Vietnam, and the military academy was built on top of a long hill about 5,000 feet in elevation, spreading from north to south. The far north was the "Nam Quan" main entrance. After the main gate, there were the headquarters, academy classes, stadium, cadet housing quarters with four long, three-floor buildings, two for each side of the hill separated by a giant grass court. The most southern end of the facility was the cadets' mess hall. All primary military training fields were in the surrounding areas.

The academic classes were scheduled during the rainy season. Most instructors were professors from the well-known universities in the country, mostly from Saigon University. I was very impressed with the modern chemical, physical, and electronic laboratories. War history and modern warfare were my most exciting classes. Guerilla warfare was a new subject at that time and was taught by American advisors based on the US Technical Manual, which was kind of ineffective counter to the current Viet Cong guerilla technic and theory changing quickly.

There were only two seasons in this area. The dry season began in November and lasted to the end of April. It was hot and dry, so all military classes and exercises took place during these months. My Class 21 also included six weeks of ranger training from the real Special Rangers Training Center down near the coastline province near Nha Trang City with the US Special Forces and ranger advisors.

The Graduations

The best memories were the graduations. They were so meaningful to me. The senior class graduating gave the juniors room to advance with a lot of privileges from the higher rank in the cadet battalion hierarchy. Therefore, our lives were getting better. Other good things we got from the senior class graduation were the former cadets visiting from the battlefields and from the different military branches. They usually wore their different military uniforms and were proud of their services. I had more chances to meet them to learn the real experiences they faced after their graduations. It was life and death valuable experiences.

However, my class graduation was still the best memory for me. It was a beautiful morning under the sunshine and the blue sky. Two hundred thirty-five cadets knelt in front of the national flag and pledged our lives to protect the country, and when we stood up, we were 235 new lieutenants. These young and well-trained officers were ready to head out in many directions like young birds flew out from the mother's nest.

There were many options and directions available for these new lieutenants of Class 21. The Air Force selected twenty-four new officers who physically qualified for pilot training requirements, then the Airborne, the Marines, the Rangers, and the Army welcomed them all.

I smelled freedom, challenges, danger, and many unknown things waiting out there, but I was still very happy to leave the academy to face a real military career in my real life.

Vietnamese National Military Academy, Main Gate

(Picture from the former TVBQGVN)

Cadets Battalion (Picture from the former TVBQGVN)

Chapter 8

KINGBEE PILOTS

-oO*Oo-

I graduated from Class 21 in 1966 with two choices resulted from the final tests for my career, as a military intelligence agent or an Air Force pilot. I picked the Air Force and was selected for pilot training in the US.

The Vietnam War was known as the helicopter's war with mobility and surprise as the keys to the battlefields. After one and a half years of training in the US, I became a Choctaw CH34 helicopter pilot. My first combat assignment was the 219th KingBees Squadron in Da Nang with special missions to the US Special Force Operations in Vietnam, Laos, and Cambodia. The squadron had more than a couple of dozen Choctaw Sikorsky CH 34s, which were very popular then.

The Choctaw was powered with a nine-radius-cylinder gas piston engine serving as a gigantic metal mass protecting pilots in the front and a enormous transmission in the back of the seats to protect pilots from behind. I really felt comfortable in the cockpit and well protected.

The heavy engine in front also helped the Choctaw dive down at a swift rate when the engine power cut down to idle. Most KingBee pilots used autorotation mode with quickly descending in an irregular individual signature pattern, like a dead leaf falling. They could also come in straight with extreme low-level flying to the LZ to avoid the enemy ground fire, surviving the most dangerous missions of insertion and extraction of the recon teams from the other side of the fence or inside the enemy activity zones.

With a mammoth body, thunderous roaring noise, and two giant A-frame landing gear trusses equipped with two prominent front landing wheels flying over the treetops, the KingBees suddenly terrified the enemy to death. The Viet Cong just had enough time to take cover and keep their heads down to the ground or run to tree trunks to hide, and the giant scary machines had long gone. The enemy would have no time to fire their weapons at them.

The US Marines used Choctaws to transport and launch the ground assault. The Navy used them as submarine hunters. CH34s were also the main US Army workhorse until switching over to the Bell UH1 Hueys.

The SOG (Studies and Observations Group) Reconnaissance Teams had engaged in the Secret Wars in the Vietnam, Laos, and Cambodia. Supposedly, by the US government, they did not legally exist.

RT Members and KingBees

The RT (Reconnaissance Team) got fully covered by air support anywhere and everyone, from the US Air Force, Army, Airborne, Marines, and Navy. However, none of them dared to take the mission of inserting and extracting the SOG RT in and out of the enemy zones or across the fence to North of DMZ, Laos, Cambodia, and Vietnam. There were only the KingBee pilots who committed to live and die with them by flying the CH34s in and out from many impossible missions.

The KingBees became the RT's angels. These pilots were their only lifesavers. The Recon teams could count on the Kingbees when they came close to death, which was the case on many missions. Their job was to collect intelligence and information from the North Vietnamese troops crossing the DMZ and moving south. These commandos also disrupted the enemy plan.

The North Vietnamese Army troops rested and slept during the day in the dense jungle to avoid being detected and wiped out by the B52 carpet bombing. All the activities took place at night so the team members could merge into the enemy troops to share their activities with them and collect information on the size of the enemy unit, their commander, their destination, and their armament. Therefore, when and if the enemy detected the Special Force RT blending in their unit, they immediately hunted down to capture or kill our team members, one by one, at any cost. At that moment, the KingBees would be called into the boiling hot LZ and be ready to go down, regardless of how dangerous it was, to pick them up and take them home.

Because of the nature of our impossible missions and the dangerous areas of our operations, the number of casualties of KingBee pilots was very high. We lost our comrades and dear friends so often. I kept my wife, Linda, in the dark from my daily military activities. She often showed her serious concern about my risky life and my hazardous military activities during my two-week tour of duty. I just cheered her up and kept moving on while the number of Kingbee pilots continued to shrink down at the alarming level.

Linda never knew that during the two week-tour-of-duty, we flew countless dangerous missions of inserting and extracting the SOG commando Reconnaissance Teams in and out the enemy line.

I invited home some very close friends for dinner with us occasionally, and later Linda kept reminding me to invite them again when she planned to prepare some favorite dishes. She didn't know some of them had been long gone from the mission impossible and never *returned to base*, but I never mentioned it to her. I talked her out of it by saying, "he is no longer with my squadron," or "he had transferred to a different place," and I thought, pretty soon, I would run out of my explanations why I could not invite those friends to have dinner with us anymore.

Chapter 9

MISSIONS IMPOSSIBLE

-oO*Oo-

KingBee Pilots and the Flight Rules

"Da Nang Tower, ...KingBee Lead."

"KingBee Lead, ...Da Nang Tower, OVER..."

"Request to taxi and take off 3 Choctaws CH34 from Whiskey 3."

"Roger KingBee. Clear to taxi 3 Choctaws from Whiskey 3."

"KingBee Lead, this is Da Nang Ground Control Tower, OVER."

"Go ahead, Da Nang Tower."

"Report your mission number."

"Mission number is unknown, OVER."

Hmm???

"KingBee Lead, repeat your mission number, OVER."

"Mission Number is unknown."

"KingBee Lead, report your destination."

"Destination is unknown."

Hmm???

After a couple of minutes of silence, the Da Nang Ground Control Tower must have verified and recognized the special out-law operations of the KingBees and responded.

"Roger, KingBee Lead. Mission number is unknown. Your destination is unknown."

"Danang Control Tower, KingBee Lead, request to take off 3 Choctaws CH34, OVER."

"KingBee Lead, this is Danang Air Tower. The airport is currently under IFR, Wind from the south-southwest, 5 miles per hour, visibility is five hundred feet, heavy rain."

"Danang Air, KingBee Lead, copied... Request Special IFR take off."

Hmm???

After a long pause of four or five minutes of silence.

"OK... KingBee Lead, acknowledge. You are cleared to take off. Take care of yourself, OVER."

"Roger, OUT."

I was stung and shocked, but Captain An led three KingBees to roll forward quickly, and in seconds the aircraft lifted off from the taxiway. He penetrated a heavy monsoon following the reflection of the wet surface of the road below and was closely trailed by two wingmen directly overhead. The rotor blades cut through the wet and heavy rain and pierced the milky sky surrounded by mountains. I asked Captain An what the *special IFR* was. He looked at me, smiled, and said... "**I F**ollow the **R**oad."

The Hai Van Pass separated Danang from Hue. The weather north and south of the pass was totally different. Rain covered the north side of the pass. The violent wind was very strong and gusty, unpredictable from the south when it smacked the mountains and bounced back to the ocean brutally like a giant tidal wave releasing pressure. This weather phenomenal often created the huge deadly vacuum that had killed many pilots by sucking their aircraft down into the water and disappeared in the ocean.

We were approaching the south of Hai Van Pass with tailwinds smashing onto the steep side of the mountain pass. It created an enormous vacuum with a very unstable air mass that could cause our Choctaw lost control and altitude suddenly. Alternatively, the inland path has enemy antiaircraft machine guns hidden under the dense canopies of the jungle on the mountainside. The open path on the sea increased the chances of being killed by rough weather, turbulence, or a strong twist of wind could pull the helicopter down into the water or slamming the aircraft into the huge sharp-toothed edges of rock walls.

Captain An led the three KingBees in climbing up to just a minimum clearance altitude along the pass due to bad weather and very low visibility. Descending to the north side a couple of hundred feet above the ground, he said that it was the safer path to FOB1, the US Airborne Forward Operations Base Camp Phu Bai.

That was the way the KingBees flying, out of the book I learned from the flight school. That was the type of mission in Vietnam Secret Wars that the KingBee pilots were assigned for daily to support the US Special Operations.

The 219th Squadron

I reported for duty to the 219th KingBees Squadron after I returned from the US flight school in late 1968. In my first month, I was assigned as a duty officer. Everything I had learned from flight school did not apply here. There was not much information on the missions. The flight leader with three or four wingmen released other flights at FOBs for every two weeks. The daily mission from Da Nang was reported to FOB1 Phu Bai or Monkey Mountain Marines Camp. Those leaders knew what they would be doing, but others had no clue.

There were only four flight leaders at that time, as many legendary names were no longer alive. These guys had extraordinary flight skills and accomplished many impossible missions before the Secret Wars took their lives. Their ultimate sacrifices kept their names alive in everyone's memory.

Most officers called each other by their first name. Military saluting was rarely used here. Uniform-wearing was not too uniform. It was not easy to become AC (Aircraft Commander). A flight leader was a far reach for most KingBee pilots unless you were the cream of the crop, having the incredible flying skill, and still alive after many challenging and impossible missions.

Some legendary pilot names were *'CowBoy,'* *'Mustachio,'* *'Rau-Kem,'* and *'Cao-Cao'* pilots who were part of the history of the KingBees.

These guys had an extraordinary skill of flying the Choctaw CH34 in the battle of the Secret Wars that no one could learn from anywhere. Not from flight school, not from a flight manual. Each of them developed his own style, his own unique technique to handle different situations to survive, rescue the Recon Team out of the deathtrap of the enemy, and help others survived until they died bravely.

Each leader's flight skill was significant, very distinctive, and recognized quickly by the RT members on the ground in life and death situations. In helpless situations, which were most recon missions, KingBees became to the RT's angels who were responding to their last hope.

First, as a co-pilot of the chase man, all I could do was to watch and learn the operations and specifically the life activities on the LZ and the maneuvering act of the leader to accomplish the mission. The leader normally came down in the seconds to the LZ from four, five thousand feet above the ground. When his landing wheels were just about to touch the ground, the team members jumped in, and the helicopter took off and got airborne in a blink of the eye before the enemy rushed in the LZ.

My crews function as the first wingman who was to be in readiness mode of action in case the lead got shot down. If that happened, the KingBee Two would come down instantly to pick up the downed screws, and the KingBee Three was forced to descend simultaneously on the LZ to pull the team, or the remainder of the team, out of the enemy's hands. KingBees did their work with the highest sense of urgency and with high-level of risk-taking. Any hesitation could lead the mission to fatal, giving the enemy slack time to be ready to attack the team and KingBees in the LZ.

It happened to me once in the A-Shaw Valley when the RT of five had been chased by at least a company of North Vietnamese troops who closed the death ring around the tall elephant grass hill during bad weather. The RT had nowhere to escape except digging deep fox holes to fight for their lives until the weather changed. Communist troops tried to overrun the hill all night long. The team fought back all night until they ran out of their ammo.

The KingBee Lead came down in the early morning when the weather was just clear enough to fly in. It was right after the enemy started the grass fire to burn the hill to kill the desperate team. Under very heavy fire, the KingBee Lead was shot down. Instantly, KingBee Two dove in from six thousand feet in autorotating mode circled very tight right about the hot LZ. KingBee Two recovered with full power and hovered right on top of the crashed KingBee to pick up the downed crew. We all got out of the enemy dead trap.

Immediately, I, the KingBee Three, approached steeply from a different direction, following KingBee Two. I quickly picked up the remaining team members with crazy machine guns firing at us and small rifles from all directions poking many holes into our Choctaw. The two KingBees swiftly flew at a very low level out of the hot LZ, one after the other. The escorting gunships sprayed their high-speed machine guns to clear out a path as a final bloody escape route while a pair of Phantom F4C destroyed the complete target with heavy bombs. The crippled Choctaw CH34 exploded into a giant fireball while smoke and fire covered the entire hill. We all got out, remarkably, altogether.

Returning to Phu Bai FOB, the team members jumped out of our helicopters first and hugged the KingBee pilots for a long silent moment before leaving us. Everyone was tired and too exhausted after the mission, but we were proud and happy we were all alive for the next day, or at least until RTB (return to base) at the end of today.

The Legendary KingBees

After about six months in battles, I became co-pilot for KingBee leads. The first lead mission was with Captain An *'Cao-Cao'*. His skills were so cool and so calm. It seemed to me that he knew what was taking place on the ground below him. Nothing down there could prevent him from completing his mission. More than nine times out of ten, the enemies fired at the KingBee crazily when extracting the RT.

The KingBee dropped the team behind or inside the North Vietnamese Army headquarters of a large unit moving from the North Viet Nam to the South along the Ho Chi Minh trails. During the daytime, the North Vietnamese troops hid and slept to avoid B52 bombings. They moved aggressively at night with heavy equipment and supplies. The Special

Forces teams were moving along at a distance to collect intelligence. This type of mission was a vital source for the CIA, reading the enemy strategy and battlefield planning to counter or avoid heavy casualties of our main forces.

The pre-mission brief, unlike in conventional war, was generally given in the last minutes before taking off, via radio after takeoff, or just when the target was in sight. There were no written procedures, no standard patterns or fixed operational formulas to be followed or applied.

The battlefield changed quickly in the last minutes according to the latest intel collected from the pilot of the Forward Air Controller (FAC), Bird Dog O1. Therefore, the final decision had to be made in the minute before landing. Captain An always told the escort gunship flight leaders of the US Marines Scarface and the US Airforce Green Hornets to pay close attention to the final split-second decision he made on the LZ. His last maneuver was executed instantaneously and surprisingly when he arrived on target; therefore, all others had to be watching him and the target very closely to support him and to avoid air collision.

Most KingBee leads had plenty of experience on how to read the enemy's mind and react in a split second skillfully, like experienced chess players. However, not all went well when you play this cat-and-mouse game daily with the enemy in their backyard. Failure to read the North Vietnamese troops' minds could cause a disaster in Insertion or Extraction RT missions. A small mistake in time or place could quickly become a total bloody game.

The Game of Death

KingBees had sacrificed at all costs to come down instantly in the heavy fire with all forces to take the team home or drop the team to alternate LZ. Secrecy, surprise, and fearlessness kept all of us alive and accomplished the mission. Basically, DO, or DIE, to save other lives was the name of this game. The game of dead or alive.

Since most missions were impossible, there were few of us alive after two to three years, and many great names grew into the KingBee legends. The RT Survival members never forget ... *"Throughout the Vietnam war, VNAF KingBee 219th was a legendary Squadron that flew countless harrowing missions of inserting the SOG commando teams behind the enemy line." (Source: Mark Austin Byrd.)*

Before I became AC (Aircraft Commander), I flew with many KingBee leads such as Major Thing, Captain Tuong, Captain Trong, Captain Thang, Captain Thu, and Captain De in the Special Operations from DMZ down to Loc Ning. I was familiar with most FOBs along the Ho Chi Minh trails. There were many missions close to or on the other side of the border of Laos and Cambodia.

Most missions in Laos were very tough. The mountain ranges were very high. The air was so dry and super-hot, the wind was very strong and gusty most of the time. It was so hot that the CH34 payload reduction was very noticeable. It was at half of the normal capacity in the mid-day so we could pick up a couple of American Special Forces instead of the whole team of five or six. The air was so thin at high altitudes, so it restricted any aggressive maneuvering to avoid enemy ground fire.

The CH34 was built in late WWII. All radios and navigation equipment were very heavy with tube type, hungry for power consumption, and built with many huge and heavy transformers. All of those located in the tail pylon section. Before the mission, we normally removed all electronic receivers, amplifiers and only kept FM and UHF to communicate with air and ground partners. The KingBee pilots' motto was *"Engine is running; blades are turning, KingBees are flying."*

We did not need to have a beacon light or position lights in the air to tell where we were relative to the enemy on the ground. The night flight formation must be kept in the darkness. Wingmen followed the hot orange fire from the exhaust of the lead or the next one on the left echelon formation.

The massive nine-cylinder engine located directly below and in the front of the cockpit was a giant mass of metal serving as an armor plate to protect the pilots. The ground fire could damage one or two cylinders, but KingBees could make it home with the rest intact. It was an incredible machine that kept us alive and allowed us to finish our jobs. The engine was hefty in front, so when a pilot cut down the throttle, the Choctaw fell at a very fast rate of descent. With skillful maneuvering, most KingBee leads created their own signature of dead leaves falling within seconds down to the LZ. The enemy, most of the time, aimed, fired, and missed.

Taking off from the LZ was a different story. It required significant technique and individual skill to keep us all alive and get out of the most dangerous areas. I got shot down with Captain Tuong in one dangerous extraction mission after the North Vietnamese troops had chased RT.

There was no way to escape, so the team selected a B52 bomb crater surrounded by tall trees as the LZ. We came in with a low-level tree-top flight. When we came over the giant fresh brown dirt crater filled with deep muddy water, the enemy shot at us from all directions. I could hear the AK-47 popping so close, and the bullets hit all over the helicopter, sound likes kids throwing rocks and gravels at the car while we were driving. The Choctaw could not hold up. The engine caught fire with a red flame curtained the front, the tail rotor failed, and we crashed the helicopter on my side in the muddy water.

The entire helicopter was sinking into water and mud. The second KingBee came down instantly. I climbed out of the right-side cockpit window and crawled along the tail pylon to get out of the deep muddy bomb crater. I saw four; five team members stand up with their AR-15s to fire back at the enemy. One team member even helped me and then other Kingbees crew members boarding the rescue helicopter and then continued shooting to stop the enemy from taking over the bomb hole.

The RT then requested A6 SkyRaiders with very close fire support to keep them safe while running downhill to be picked up from a different LZ.

After returning to FOB for refueling, I volunteered to fly back to the target again. Tuong and I took the grounded CH34 without a fuel gauge and transmission oil pressure indicator. We returned to the battlefield, along with two wingmen. We came in downwind to a very narrow and confined spot that was cleared out by the SkyRaiders' gun run. We used the helicopter blade tips to chop off small tree branches to fit the CH34 affectingly under towered tree canopies to hide from the enemy at the uphill.

Even the landing wheels had not touched the ground, the remaining team already jumped in, and we took off in the same direction we just got in. The team unleashed ammo and hand grenades down to the areas where the North Vietnamese troops ran after them.

More than a dozen holes were poking through our helicopter cabin, but none hit the blades. Captain Tuong then explained to me later that we came in downwind, which surprised the enemy. The smoke and fire from our downed helicopter told them the wind direction, and they learned that the pilot should land and take off headwind and were ready for us with machine guns waiting. The remaining team members were saved, and we lost one CH34. Everyone was exhausted. We all returned to base. Another day, another battle with different challenges.

In heavy trees and bushes covering the jungle, both the North Vietnamese Army and our Recon Team rested and slept to avoid being detected by airplanes. They moved quietly to the south at night along the Ho Chi Minh trails network. During the nighttime, the jungle was clean and pure nature. Any smell from modern society such as cigarettes, aftershave lotion, soap, or odor spray would be detected clearly and easily from the other side.

The team was isolated in solitary tents for four to five days without any connection to the outside, for security purposes. The team also unloaded and cleared out those smells before insertion into the jungle for secret recon missions. Any little mistake made could cost lives and suffering of team members and disaster to the mission.

The Sacrifices

KingBees were the last option after all else failed. After discovering the team members present, the North Vietnamese Army made a big chase to hunt them down. The team ran as quickly as they could, calling Forward Air Control (FAC) for an emergency pick up. KingBees were on standby at the Forward Operations Base (FOB) and ready for the extraction mission regardless of any situation or condition. The team reported their position with an orange panel from their jungle hat or with a small flat mirror. They continued to run away from the enemy. FAC guided the running team to the nearest confined area as a possible LZ to be picked up.

The team then used their firepower to slow down the enemy approaching the selected LZ. KingBees instantly dove down to separate the team from the enemy, hovering and turning the right side toward the team and dropping quickly down to the ground as soon as possible. The enemy unloaded all the firepower they had toward the KingBee and the team to hold them down. The most enemy fire came from the co-pilot side.

KingBee co-pilots who survived after a couple of years of these experiences became AC. Before descending to land in the LZ, I always checked and set my co-pilot's shoulder harness to the LOCKED position. Just in case..., he got shot, his body needed to be tied to the back seat to avoid leaning forward to the cyclic control just for the safety and the survival of the rest. KingBee co-pilots took the most hits from enemy firepower and had less defense due to the lack of machine guns on their side of the aircraft.

KingBee co-pilots also had the most casualties from the US Special Forces Operations. Since CH34 has only one passenger door on the right side, the same side with AC (Aircraft Commander), most extraction missions were called in the last minute after the enemy discovered the RT was penetrating in their moving units. The team then ran as fast as possible to keep a reasonable distance from the enemy and make room for the KingBee to land at a selected confined area between the team and the enemy. Therefore, the pilot automatically turned his co-pilot side to the enemy and his side with the passenger door facing our team to pick them up. Co-pilots got shot most the time in the hot LZs.

In my first several months flying as co-pilot, I never recognized ground fire. There were many radio channel communications over my helmet, besides the intercoms. FM channel from the team on the ground and with other KingBees, with the FAC, the escorting gunners, the RT; UHF from F4 and SkyRaiders. The first time I heard and at the same time recognized there was ground fire flashing from thick bushes nearby my site on LZ; I squeezed the radio trigger on the cyclic to report "Heavy ground fire from nine o'clock." My AC responded calmly, "Ignore the report, keep radio channel open." I learned later that KingBees only reported ground fire from machine guns or bigger guns, not from AK-47s or rifles.

The Irregular Warriors

Unlike a regular unit, RT never used smoke signals to indicate their location. The KingBee lead frequently found them after coming down close to the ground. Team members got in the helicopter before the landing gears touched the ground. In some special missions, RT was dressed and equipped exactly the same as the North Vietnamese Army. They used a secret signal agreed upon before the mission, which became crucial in a life or death situation. The left-hand sleeve rolled up, and AK-47 held on the same side was a secret signal in one mission in Laos.

The North Vietnamese troops discovered the US Special Forces members had been following them. The enemy started searching for the team members in the early morning. One was killed, and four escaped. A battle broke out. KingBees were called in to extract the four remaining team members out of the deathtrap circle surrounded by the enemy. The KingBee door gunner quickly shot and killed the first team of six before they boarded the helicopter. Within seconds, there were our four surviving members with their left-hand sleeves rolled up, and AK-47s were held on that same side.

The KingBee lead's door gunner, who had been in this secret war battle for a long time, said it was easy to recognize them by looking at their body size and the way they handled their rifles while they ran toward the helicopter. Our team members never pointed the rifles toward to helicopter while boarding. They always watched their back and their sides and ready to fire back the enemy before jumping onto the aircraft. With his instant actions, this door gunner had saved the lives of KingBee's crews and RT members who were within seconds from death.

Chapter 10

MORE MISSIONS IMPOSSIBLE

-oO*Oo-

The North Vietnamese troops moved from north of DMZ to Laos and Cambodia borders along the Ho Chi Minh trails in a short time after signing the Geneva Accords. The US used F4C fighters to destroy bridges, roads, and supply posts along the trails to stop the communist troops, weapons, and foods moving south. However, there was not much effective because the North Vietnamese Army had many engineering units to repair the damages right away. The communist troop also opened a new trail quickly under well-covered jungle canopies to make the detour if the bombing damages were unrepairable. The North Vietnamese Army continued their southward journey to its military tactical points or its major destinations in South Vietnam to prepare for the larger battles.

Air Force C119s equipped with electronic heat sensor devices had also been deployed to detect the enemy's body heat and cooking flames in evenings along the network trails. It was only working from the beginning; however, later, the enemy troops spread out very thin to rest at days and moved quietly at nights. The B52s occasionally called in and laid carpet bombings in some dense jungle believed to be the enemy troops' highly concentrated areas; however, the enemy got the secret intelligence in advance as soon as B52s took off from Guam or U-Tapao, Thailand, and spread out or moved away.

Boots on the ground with Special Operations was the real solution to that problem. The small teams of the fearless commandos volunteered to handle the dangerous task. Together with other supporting units from four branches of the US Armed Forces, they made up this Special Operations of the Secret Wars in Vietnam, the wars behind and inside the enemy's lines. These were very risky wars, but it was the most effective way in military tactic and strategy. The small reconnaissance team members have sacrificed their lives to save thousands of our regular troops.

Special Forces were dropped in along Ho Chi Minh trail networks to follow the North Vietnamese troops, to collect information, to disrupt their plan, and to slow down their schedule to reach the target destination. Those operation missions were the vital elements for our regular troops in making the proper important strategic military decisions and having enough time in preparation for the coming battlefields before the communists attacked us.

The Special Forces Recon Team and its operations entered many shapes and forms of the Secret Wars. The battle was like chess games, the games of death. Each side was gauging what the other side was thinking and reacting in order to act and to counteract. Therefore, there were no conventional procedures and operations like a traditional war.

The Military Chess Games

Since 1969, there were too many North Vietnamese troops that moved to post on the critical strategic points along the Ho Chi Minh trails on the highland center of Vietnam. The recon team missions were very tough and riskier, going behind the enemy's control area. The operations changed to many different forms. The missions became complicated and engaged multiple targets simultaneously. We had a real recon team and a dummy recon team for the same mission.

KingBee One and KingBee Two became the insertion helicopters for two different LZs, Alpha and Bravo at the same time. We even didn't know which one was real or which one was fake until the last minutes. I was the KingBee Two of that inserting mission. We were instructed to land on LZ A, to drop the "Team," dummy team, down along with a pallet of firecrackers. This fake team and firecracker pallet simulated the sound of battle, like gunfire from rifles, machine guns, and rockets, and the team members to lure the communists into a distraction area. In the meantime, KingBee One dropped a different team, the real team, in LZ B without enemy resistance.

There was another type of mission. It was to play in the Low-and-High Altitudes tactic. Near the LZ, one KingBee would fly at a low-level near the treetops while the other KingBees flew at a high-level altitude for at least thirty minutes in the same area so the enemy could start their guessing games of where the inserting target would be. All eyes paid attention in the sky, all ears were busy listening around from all directions, but no one knew that our RT had already walked on the ground in the jungle from a different target LZ nearby.

The scariest mission that I was assigned was to drop one man on the Ho Chi Minh trail in the middle of the day without any weapon. He dressed like a French plantation worker. The LZ was too open. The trail was big and wide open. There was no sign of any human on the ground at daytime. I landed on the trail with many fresh tire tracks from heavy trucks or bigger vehicles packed down just a night before. We dropped the man down with his bicycle. When we took off, he rode on his bicycle and pedaled along the trail, exactly like the French plantation man doing his daily job. However, our plantation man's job was to tap the phone line and to record telephone conversations of the top-level communist commanders when he had a chance.

Three days later, I came in and picked him up from the trail about twenty miles north from where I had dropped him off. I did not know what else he did during those scary days, but he looked calm and remained intact as a French plantation worker.

The southern part of Ho Chi Minh trails along the Cambodia border was wider and well packed with heavy trucking traffic; however, there was no indication of any presence of the enemy troops at all. Instead of dropping RT in,

KingBees dropped camouflaged variation signal sensing antennas along the main trails. These signal receivers read and recorded a lot of foot traffics at night along a stretch of trail over the past several nights.

The RT was inserted by KingBees successfully without encountering any resistance from the North Vietnamese troops. After days and nights of close observation on many different areas of the trail from the team members, it turned out the herd of elephants had been in these areas in the last couple of days, and the antennas had picked up the vibration, mistaking it with vehicles and human foot traffics.

No damage was done. The enemy troops were still moving south, and so their supply continued trucking at nights along the Ho Chi Minh trails. And there was no trace of human presence in these wide-open trails.

The Food and Arms Battles

Food and arms were the two most important elements to keep the North Vietnamese troops alive and fighting. Therefore, the RT had to disrupt their storages and resupply bases along Ho Chi Minh trails. There was at least a half-dozen BAs (Base Areas) along the Ho Chi Minh trails to support the North Vietnamese troops moving south.

KingBees inserted five-member RT to an LZ nearby the major food storage camp well dug in the hillside of the U-shape mountaintop. Their mission was to estimate the volume of rice and destroy the food supply of the North Vietnamese troops. It took the team a couple of days to reach the target because of many steep hills, very dark jungle, and many enemies in these supply camp areas.

The emergency extraction was then called in after the team members were discovered and chased by the enemy base camp guards. The team ran for days away from the target of the rice bunkers, but I could still spot from the air a white stream of rice continued running down from the dirt hole believed to be the rice bunker's entrance and disappeared into the dark green jungle without a trace.

The Cobra gunships came in to break the North Vietnamese soldiers from reaching the team members. KingBee lead came down to the other side of the mountain in a very tight confined area to scoop them up and flew away while the gunships still made a couple low passes with its rocket launchers to destroy the remainder of the rice bunker. The successful mission had caused a serious shortage of food supply to slow down the North Vietnamese troops arriving at the pre-planned destinations.

The KingBee's mission to success relied on the instant surprise, quick action, and no hesitation regardless of how much dangerous the situation would be on the ground because the only chance to make it was within the first minute of breakout. Afterward, the deathtrap was waiting for us to come down, and the opportunity for the team members' survival was very, very, slim to none.

The Unusual Rescue Mission

One time I was at FOB #1 Phu Bai. I received a mission to *pick up* a lost man. He was the last survived of an American Special Forces recon team, who had been run off for days out of enemy hands. The subject was described as a white male taller than six feet and was chased the whole night by the local communists. He was in black pajamas and armed with an AK-47, and last estimated coordinates were somewhere in the hilly thin woody terrain about ten miles west from the South Vietnamese local firebase. My job was to go to the area immediately to find that single man to pick him up.

I arrived at the target within forty-five minutes in the very early morning. I circled around and couldn't find any single man in the thin jungle. After searching around and waiting to "rendezvous" the gunship's escort, I went to an open grassy area with small trees. I spotted out one person running quickly, pointing the AK-47 backward toward four or five smaller guys chasing him from behind.

The gun escort of the mission didn't have enough time to be on target at the time I arrived. I saw the guy taller than the elephant grass, and I believed he was my subject of the mission.

I flew down and turned my gunner side to the people chasing him. I told my gunner to shoot at them to create distance for the single guy to run further to the other side of the grass field. I made one more circle over the target then came back. Sure enough, the single guy reversed his hat, showing a small orange panel upward. I came down to pick him up. He barely made. My crew chief dragged his upper body onto the floor. His feet were still hung over the doorway in the air when we got airborne.

I landed on FOB #1 Phu Bai, and I saw the guy was in bad shape. He had no bullets in his AK-47 and just pointed his rifle backward to scare his pursuers to slow them down. I shut down the engine and walked out of the Choctaw. He held me tight for a long moment. His eyes were tearing, and his face was covered by black mud. He said slowly, "You...saved...my...life...KingBee." And sluggishly walked away.

No Body Retrieving

In the late 1960s, there were several Special Forces members captured by the communists. The communists learned how to counter the Special Forces' tactics. We received the report that the remaining recon team had been found in a confined area, west of Kontum, near Dak To area. The KingBees were ready to take off anytime, waiting for the final signal.

When we arrived over the target, we saw four human bodies lying in an open area. The LZ was very quiet, indicating no communist activity. The FAC flew a low pass to verify whether the humans were alive or dead while the KingBee's lead was waiting to come down.

The final information the FAC received confirmed that four dead bodies were wearing the missing team's uniform. That was against the Special Forces' mission. We never picked up the dead bodies, only the wounded members. However, the communists didn't know that rule. They set a boobytrap to wait for us to come down and kill us. The KingBee lead came down halfway before receiving the order to *abort the mission*. It saved KingBee crews and a lot of people that supported the mission. We returned to base very late at night. We all drank to celebrate. The last vital information had saved our lives.

The Medivac Mission

I flew the rescue and Medivac (Medical Evacuation) missions with Choctaw CH34 for the Airborne division in the Khe Sanh battle in 1971. The US Marines, Airborne, Cavalry, Navy, Air Force, and the Vietnamese Army, Airborne, Marines, and Rangers fought the North Vietnamese with very heavy mobile artilleries at the high points along both sides of the big valley where Route 9 ran from Southern Laos to the Dong Ha District of Quang Tri Province.

The Khe Sanh airstrip became the busiest, with all kinds of air and ground traffics. It took me almost thirty minutes in a holding pattern before I could land the helicopter and report to the Combat Base Headquarters under the ground just off the runway.

Since the base was surrounded by the North Vietnamese Army and Viet Cong troops for many days, all aircraft were forced to hug close to the runway for safety before making the final approach.

C123s or C130s dropped the airborne supplies and ammunition pallets from high altitudes with parachutes. Some landed outside the defense lines and went into the wrong hands. There were very few people on the ground surface. Most of the troops were under the bunkers, in the deep tunnels, or in foxholes due to the enemy's artillery and mortar shells pounding the base at any time, day and night.

My first mission was to supply the emergency ammunition and pick up the wounded Airborne soldiers from Hilltop 31, deep inside Laos border. After a short weather briefing, here came the military intelligence with the most critical and vital information on the status of enemy activities in the battlefields. The enemy mobile artillery positions were clearly marked in red color all over the map, covering almost every hillside from high points of both sides of the valley.

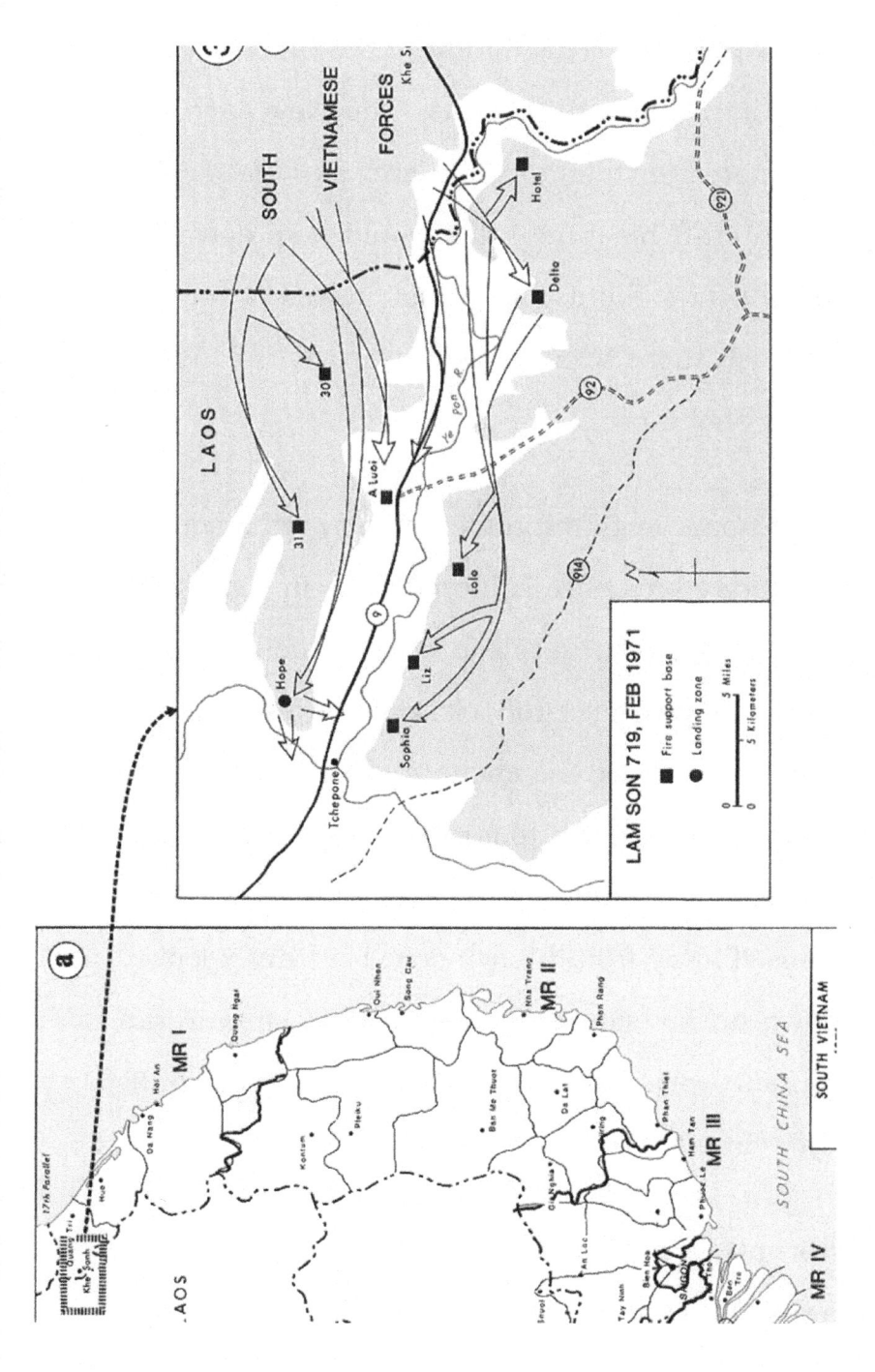

(Picture of Khe Sanh 71 Battle Map from US Army)

I decided to fly in the middle of the valley to avoid antiaircraft machine guns. The Navy artillery dominated the high-altitude level, and the enemy's antiaircraft machine guns would take down the low-altitude flights, so I just played with luck because there was no way to avoid the risk of being shot down.

After about forty minutes of flying, we headed to the target area. The Hilltop 31 was in sight, with bare brown dirt and deep bomb craters all over. I asked my co-pilot to look down on his side and watch closely for the enemy's ground fire while I started diving down to land on the narrow LZ. He immediately jumped onto the center console to keep himself away from his window. I instantly looked down on my side and spotted many antiaircraft rounds exploding with dozens of black smoke puffs very close to the bottom of our helicopter.

Abruptly, I made a steep bank to the right to get away from the shooting pattern of the machine guns from the ground. I saw in front of my eyes at least three rounds penetrating up to the center radio control panel where my co-pilot just jumped his butts on. One went through, the second one punched a big hole, slicing the metal like an open mushroom. The third one just pushed up the thicker metal case and curved up like a young mushroom, just popping up from underneath the radio control panel.

My FM and intercom went dead. Black smoke and a bad electronic burning smell came out from the radio panel. The helicopter shook violently with severe vibrations. Instead of diving down for an emergency landing, I pulled up to gain altitude to get out of the shooting range of the antiaircraft machine guns.

My co-pilot was so nervous. He wanted to jump out of the helicopter. His face turned white like a dead man. I locked up my shoulder harness, turned my face to him and locked up his also, just in case one of the pilots got shot the body would not lean to the cyclic control that would kill everyone. At the same time, the AWAC (Airborne Warning and Control) was broadcasting an urgent alert through the VHF emergency channel... "Warning! Warning! SAM... SAM... SAM..." The whole sky went out of control. All aircrafts were changing altitude, diving, climbing, breaking left, and breaking right to avoid the detected surface-to-air missiles (SAM) that had been fired into the airspace.

I gave my hand signal to my co-pilot and ordered him to open his window. He hesitated for a moment while I opened mine. He then understood that we needed to vent out the smoke from the burning cockpit or we would be suffocated by the smoke and toxic fumes.

As I was making a 180-degree turn, he raised his arms up to ask where we were going. I responded to him by pointing my finger in the direction of where we took off from. He was relieved.

I asked him to take control of the helicopter for a moment so I could check the radio to see what the problem was. I switched the knobs back and forth, hoping to hear any static or any noise from the intercom. It was all dead. I tapped my boots on the floor to communicate with my crew's chief. In a second, I saw his hand raised up with his thumb down. The intercom was out and surely dead.

I called the escorting gunships on the UHF radio to inform them with hope they could hear me, that I must return to base as soon as possible or make an emergency landing somewhere on my return route in case the cockpit fire burned out of control and the vibration became too severe and too dangerous to continue flying.

The electronic burning continued, and the smell worsened, but there was no safe place along this valley to land. Suddenly the alert of naval artillery came in repeatedly via the VHF emergency channel warning all aircraft in the area to get out of 8,000 to 12,000 feet altitude immediately. I took the control back from my co-pilot and went down to 6,000 feet and then 5,000 feet. There were several tanks on Route 9 that I saw earlier when I came in. Now they were burning with very dark black smoke rising in the air. A Cobra and a Huey had crashed on the roadside.

Many flashing lights flared up from the hillsides as the enemy machines fired at me. They missed. I dropped my altitude lower and lower, flying right over the treetops following the creek.

I looked at the bullet holes on the radio console and believed my rotor blades got hit by at least one round penetrating through to the cockpit ceiling and caused the low-frequency vibration. I flew with very slow speed to reduce the violent shaking and finally, I made an emergency landing at the west end of the runway of Khe Sanh Base. The ambulance and fire trucks followed me tightly while I taxied off the runway to a dirt pad nearby.

Many big bullets punched big holes in the nose section. Two hit the trailing edge of the rotor blades. Luckily, none hit the two pallets of ammunition in the cargo section.

My mission was aborted, and sadly, the wounded Airborne soldiers were still on the Hilltop 31.

The Unknown Heroes

I left 219th KingBee Squadron in late 1971 for Chinook pilot training in the US after two and a half years of excitement from the most dangerous missions. I was lucky to be alive from those impossible missions and became an aircraft commander and a flight leader. I never forgot those extremely brave pilots who made the KingBees legendary in the Secret Wars. Since all our KingBees' missions were UNKNOWN and all KingBees' operations and destinations were also UNKNOWN, those brave KingBee pilots, who died to save our friends' lives and some are still alive and living somewhere, were also UNKNOWN. It was too sad.

However, KingBees were unknown but not forgettable. I ran into a war article written by J. Stryker Meyer, an RT survived member, who knew and respected those KingBees, and I proudly repeated by copying his statement as below.

"When I die, if the Lord gives me a moment to reflect before I breathe my last breath, my first thoughts will be not of my loved ones, nor my children.

I'll reflect on and thank God for Sau, Hiep, Phouc, Tuan, Hung, Son, Quang, Chau, Cau and Minh. Captains Tuong and Thinh and lieutenants Trung and Trong will follow them in my thoughts. Then, I'll think of my loving wife, our talented and unique children, and our folks.

Why the Vietnamese men before my loved ones? Without the courage, strength and fearless verve as combatants in America's secret war in Southeast Asia, I wouldn't have returned to the United States."

And furthermore...

"Today, on the 25th anniversary of the fall of Saigon, I'll pause to salute those warriors, men most Americans will never hear about, including the more than 3 million US troops sent to South Vietnam during America's longest and costliest war." (J. Stryker Meyer, a North County Times staff writer, served in the Special Forces from 1968 to 1970.)

After the dark day of April 30, 1975, many former KingBees spread out too many places on earth. The lucky few escaped Viet Nam a day or two before the fall of Saigon and many escaped at the day of the surrender from the newly formed South Vietnamese government. And some, like me, escaped even a day after the new South Vietnamese government had collapsed.

"All soldiers should lay down the guns... All pilots must return airplanes to home base... All airports are closed... No airplane is allowed to take off..." That was an insulting and betraying surrendering order unconditionally from the newly formed government broadcasting by the South Vietnamese government radio network and via UHF Aviation Emergency Channel during April 29th, 1975.

I ignored the surrender order and took the Chinook to escape out of the country twice. The first time at night on the 29th of April was failed due to the bad weather on the ocean and heavy rain along the coastline. I got caught. My two flight crew members were escorted back to Can Tho Air Base.

I escaped the next day again, on April 30, with my lucky Chinook tail number "000" after the communists attempting to take over the base. I was one of the lucky few who landed on Con Son Island, picked up my family along with some eighty women and children left behind in the last hopeless minutes, and finally landed on the USS *Okinawa* helicopter aircraft carrier, out in the international waters, a day after the surrender order.

The unfortunate KingBees were stuck with their lives in hell for five or ten years in the communist re-education camps. They paid a dearly cost after surviving many dangerous missions that only a few pilots could do, and who were brave enough to accept the duty of the impossible missions and gave a big sacrifice to all.

Most Americans never hear about them, only the surviving team members of the Special Operations still remember the KingBees, whom they lived and died with. Here was one of the many respectful comments from a former team member *"The best of those pilots were selected for the elite, top-secret 219th Special Operations Squadron. As the secret war grew in size, the 219th spread its wings along with the expanded operations. By January 1968, there were six*

Forward Operating Bases in South Vietnam, all supported by KingBees". (Wrote by John Stryker Meyer from *Soldier of Fortune* Magazine)

Due to the lack of spare parts and the high requirement of maintenance, The CH34 Choctaws were forced to retire and were replaced by the Bell Helicopter UH1 in 1971. I left the KingBees 219th Squadron for the CH47 Chinook pilot training in the US after my two and a haft years of services to the SOG RT. The rest of the KingBee pilots and crew members continued the dangerous missions with the smaller and much more fragile Hueys until after the fall of Viet Nam in of 1975.

After graduation from the Chinook flight school and the US Armed Forces Instruction Pilot, I served as a member of the Staff Squadron of *Thien Bang* 241st stationed in Phu Cat Air Base. I flew as a combat pilot, instructor pilot, and test pilot in the center of Viet Nam and finally, a couple of years later, moved down to Can Tho Air Base in southern Viet Nam with the new 249th Chinook Squadron with code name *Manh Long*. It was the last air base of my last flight out in 1975 with my lucky Chinook triple zero tail number. However, I will never forget those exciting days as a KingBee pilot from many impossible missions.

The Unforgettable Pilots

Since our missions were highly classified and participants in the Vietnam Secret Wars, there was not a lot of records disclosed to the public, and very few pilots and team members had opportunities to take pictures or jot down any notes of those days. There was not enough time to socialize or do those things either. And it was not important to anyone. We lived daily with full excitement and facing life or death. Our lives were counted by days, not years. In fact, we did not exist, supposedly, according to the government records.

After April 1975, most lucky South Vietnamese pilots escaped Viet Nam and spread out all over the world with new lives. Many were in the US, Canada, and Australia. The unlucky few left behind ended up in re-education camps in many remote jungles all over Viet Nam. They had paid extremely costs after the war.

For the American servicemen, it was the thankless war; for the Vietnamese, the war was senseless and destructive to their country. However, we did not make that decision. Our superiors made it. This was the terrible and the result from the deadly wrong decisions of the Viet Nam War. However, we all had performed our duties well, we completed our missions and suffered from it as the soldiers.

We fought bravely, we sacrificed greatly, and we survived toughly from the war. The most important thing to me was not being forgotten from each other who had given up their lives to save others and to keep the rest alive. Here was a great observation from other surviving team members.

"Today, there are former SOG Green Berets and indigenous team members who are alive only through the heroics and flying skills of KingBee pilots. I'm one of those fortunate men. But, few of us realized at the time that while our tours of duty in SOG were generally for one year -- the KingBee pilots flew the deadly missions across the fence for eight years -- if they survived." (Wrote by John Stryker Meyer from *Soldier of Fortune* Magazine)

Although not many Americans knew the enormous sacrifice from the KingBee pilots and the SOG RT in the Secret Wars we fought. Many had died, and the lucky few survived. And the KingBees were not forgotten by those survivors from the war and by these RT members ... *"I'll never forget it,"* Watkins said in a recent interview with SOF. *That KingBee was the best sight in the world."*

Another team member said, *"There are so many stories of daring-do on the part of the KingBees. There are legends among their pilots... I can tell you that when a team was on the ground, the sweetest sound they heard on the radio was when a KingBee pilot would say, 'KingBee go down now,' as the pilot spiraled-down to the team under a hail of fire. Some KingBees didn't make it back."*

By John Stryker Meyer / *Soldier of Fortune* Magazine

In respect to those who did not *"return to base"* from your impossible missions, I am humbly saluting you, who gave all and we all just gave some. Rest in peace.

Chapter 11

CHINOOK OPERATIONS

-oO*Oo-

The ten-year terrible war in Viet Nam, from 1964 to 1975, was exactly in my full military service time. I entered the military when the American War started and was out as the war ended. There were many names for this war, the Second Indochina War, the American War, the Vietnam War, or even the Vietnam Conflict. One thing for sure, it was not the Vietnam War because the Americans gradually withdrew the US ground forces in 1972 and declared "Vietnamization" of the war.

Beginning in 1972, the US started withdrawing from many tactical air bases and left the Chinook helicopters behind, along with spare parts and equipment for the Vietnamese Air Force. The Thien Bang 241st Chinook squadron was formed and took over the heavy-lift helicopters in Phu Cat Air Base to support many battles of the III Corp from Pleiku, Ban Me Thuot, to the coastal provinces. I was appointed to be the training officer and test pilot for my new unit after returning from the US.

At the same time, the US advisory program was quickly boosted up to provide one advisor per unit in VNAF, from logistics, maintenance, to combat operations. The intention was to provide the Vietnamese unit commanders the American advice and support; however, the Vietnamese and American officers never worked well together. Mainly they do not understand each other, and neither side wanted to make any effort by approaching this cold feeling and boring subject.

Unlike the Special Forces RT team members, American advisors did not understand even a simple Vietnamese common word, never bothered to understand the local culture, customs, and behaviors. They operated in totally different daily working schedules and were in their different world but fighting the same war, the Vietnam War with Vietnamization.

Robert Morris was our Thien Bang squadron advisor. He was a captain and a Chinook pilot who came in without an office or a desk for him in my squadron. I believed the Thien Bang squadron commander did not want to have a desk for Bob in his office; neither did other officers. Bob came to the squadron at 7:30 a.m. on his first day and every day afterward. There were no squadron officers at that earlier morning except the officer on duty. Most pilots in daily missions were down at the aircraft's parking to do preflight inspections and to be ready to head out for the scheduled missions. Bob did not know what to do, whom to talk with, or where to sit down.

Bob saluted me when I saw him. I returned his military respect even knowing he might not recognize my rank. I introduced myself as Captain Nguyen Con, training officer of the squadron. He said he was the squadron advisor and would like to see the commander. I told him that the squadron commander expected to see him after he got out the morning briefing at the base commander's office.

Bob entered my office and asked me where I wanted his desk to be. I said, "Oh... The commander will tell you where. I guess it shall be in his office, not mine," and then my boss suddenly showed up at the door and told me to have Bob share the office with me. I did not understand why, but I had no objection. Bob seemed to be a nice guy and a well-groomed officer. Bob ended up having more interactions and activities with me than any other staff members of the squadron. He felt like he was my advisor, not my boss.

I showed Bob around the operations, the training program, and the flight safety, even though my boss never told me to do anything with Bob. I introduced him to other key officers of my squadron, but no one said more than "Hello" and "Goodbye" to Bob. I had daily flight training and did not know how Bob could handle his duty without me in the squadron of which he was the advisor. I knew he would feel very lonely without me.

Bob saw a group of crew members just returned from Pleiku after two weeks TDY (Temporary Duty Assignment). Those crew members were exhausted and looked to be in bad shape. Bob suddenly asked me, "Captain Nguyen, why do your pilots have long hair and do not shine their shoes?" I did not respond to Bob until we were in my office. I told him that unlike the US Army in the training class, all Vietnamese aviation units were in the air force; therefore, pilots usually got a little more flexibility than in the army. Further, we were in combat operations, not in training school, my boss did not wish to apply very rigid rules to his pilots, but he focused rather on flight skills and mission performance. Our motto is *"to get the job done and to keep the crews alive."* Bob did not say a word. I then followed up "Bob, remember… you only stay here for a year, and then you will return to your family in your beautiful country. Contrarily, these young people shall stay here and fight this war for life… or death. I do not want to be really hard on them either."

A couple of weeks later, Bob found out that many pilots in my squadron were flying without gloves. He acted with excitement like Columbus just discovered the American continent! I cooled him down and told him that the supply department did not have flight gloves for my pilots so they must fly with bare hands. He called someone on his advisory channel and told me that there were plenty of supplies of flight suits, helmets, and gloves. I said, "Let's go down to the supply and check it out."

Bob was surprised when he saw all the gloves in the supply room were large and extra-large sizes. I asked the supply officer, "Where are the small sizes?" The answer was, "We are currently out of the small sizes." I told Bob that it was the same answer for years.

"What are the most Vietnamese pilots' sizes?" He asked me.

"Most are small, few are large," I answered.

"What is your size?" He disappointedly asked me.

"Small." I pulled out my pair from my leg pocket and showed him.

"Where did you get them?"

"I will show you *where* after we got out of here."

Bob and I went directly to town afterward, and I showed him where I bought my size small gloves. They were from the black market because I could not wear extra-large gloves to flight. It was too dangerous by not feeling exactly where the fingers at in the huge gloves. There were many small-size flight gloves displayed in the black market. Bob then learned something else about the different face of the war. He told me he never knew this, and no one would if I had not shown him. I asked Bob if he would guess how the small-size flight gloves got out from the supply department to the black market? Bob said, "I do not know." I replied, "Me, either."

The longer we worked together, the better we understood each other. Bob Morris was serving the second tour in Vietnam. His first one was a Chinook pilot for the Aviation unit of the 101st Airborne. Bob showed me the picture of his beautiful wife in Texas and his father living in Fort Worth. We had coffee breaks and occasionally lunched together during his first month on duty. I introduced my wife Linda and our three children to Bob, and he showed some interest in Vietnamese foods and culture. Slowly and gradually, we became friends.

I told Bob that the squadron's commander and I were the KingBee pilots who flew for the US special recon teams until 1971. Flying Chinook missions were much easier and less exciting than many missions we flew along the Ho Chi Minh trails or crossing the borders to the north of DMZ, Laos, or Cambodia. Bob was very eager to fly with me. He pulled out a letter signed by the Vietnamese Air Force Commander in Chief saying he had the permission to fly the Vietnamese Chinook helicopter as a pilot. I took him out for his first flight to gauge and refresh his skill level before releasing Bob to fly a combat mission with my pilots, even for just a couple of missions.

Bob handled the control to show me his first performance in the traffic patterns and landed on a specified spot I picked. I asked Bob to fly exactly and precisely as it was supposed to be as an AC. I pointed my finger to the flight instruments to show him the climbing rate should be 500 feet per minute during the climbing, not 510 or 550; all needles of the gauges should indicate right on correct numbers as required. Bob could hardly land precisely on the center of the letter marked on the runway.

I took the control and demonstrated to Bob how I could fly a Chinook easily and precisely. I was flying a complete traffic pattern, talking to him, and pointed my finger to all flight instruments with all pointers maintained precisely at the numbers I told him they were supposed to be. I landed right on the center of the big letter marked at the end of the runway. I asked my crew chief to open the ramp. I showed Bob the center of the Chinook was lined up with the centerline of the runway from the aircraft nose to the tail, and that was what I expected my pilots' flying skill level before I released them as an aircraft commander.

I took off and asked Bob to fly one more pattern without SAS *(**S**tabilization **A**ugmentation **S**ystem)*. The Chinook flew not smoothly as I expected. Like most Chinook pilot, Bob got a tough time to control the helicopter without SAS engaged and assisted. I told him that a combat AC pilot must have the adequate flying skill to handle the mission without SAS.

Taxing the Chinook was a challenging maneuver because it was a four-wheel aircraft with the two front fixed wheels and swiveling rear wheels. Only the left side of the rear wheel had powered steering capability with a very sensitive control knob on the center console between the two pilots.

Chinook pilot had both hands busy while taxing the helicopter with the right hand on cyclic and the other on the steering wheel knob while power control, collective pitch and radio communication must be constantly maintained.

The rear rotor system created up to seventy percent of the uplifting force; therefore, when the rear section got too much power, the rear wheels lost the ground contact and the friction to the ground, then the steering wheel could be de-phased. The steering wheel then became ineffective, the aircraft could go slightly airborne suddenly and slap its rear section into any objects nearby, and the aircraft crashed and burned in many cases.

Bob had a difficult time taxing the Chinook along the narrow taxiways. I showed him how to have positive control of the steering by reducing the power on the collective control pitch and pull back the cyclic to gently increase the weight onto the ground. He was surprised by my skill, knowledge, and instructions.

Bob stopped the Chinook in front of the U-shaped bunkers and attempted the shutdown procedure. I told him, "Not here," and pointed my finger to one of the empty bunkers.

"In there?" he asked.

"Yes, Bob, like the rest parking inside the bunkers or the enemy's mortar will destroy it at night."

"Are you kidding me, Captain Nguyen? Where is the tractor?" He asked.

"No, there is no tractor here. I asked you to taxi backward into the bunker, Bob."

"I never taxi backward, and I do not think I can do that," Bob strongly refused.

"OK. Then I will do it," I looked at Bob and replied.

I asked my crew chief to raise the ramp up halfway and clear the rear side. I prepared to back in the bunker.

I slightly raised the nose section up, and the Chinook rolled slowly back onto the center of the bunker. I set it down, reduced the power, and started the shutdown procedure. Bob was stunned and amazed at what I did but said nothing.

We walked back to the squadron office. It was quite a long distance, but we did not have vehicles to pick us up, and the conversation was on.

"Where you learn how to fly the Chinook?" Bob asked me.

"Fort Rucker, Alabama."

"When did you become an IP (instructor pilot)?"

"I graduated the US Armed Forces MOI class 1972," I said.

"What is MOI?" Bob asked.

"It is *Method of Instruction Pilot*; the course was conducted by the FAA and flight training by US Instructor Pilots."

"Where did you learn to taxi backward?"

"From taxiing forward," I replied.

Bob did not respond, so I explained that the Chinook body is a big rectangular box with four wheels on the ground and two rotor systems in the air, front and back. It could be taxied either way.

"How was my flight?" Bob changed the subject.

"I will have a debriefing with you in the office," I said.

My debriefing contained some important details and analyzing of Bob's flying. I told Bob although he had permission to fly a Chinook in my squadron, it did not mean he was qualified automatically to handle the combat mission as my squadron special operations and qualifications requirements. Bob asked me seriously when I think he could. I told him it would take a couple more training flights with me.

"Why are you in a hurry, Bob?"

"I want to be able to fly at least one combat mission," Bob responded.

"For what?" I asked.

"For meeting the minimum requirement of a squadron advisor."

"I see. But I cannot release you to fly in the battlefield until you passed the combat mission check flight."

"Ok, Captain Nguyen," Bob replied.

The First Combat Mission

I flew with Bob at least two to three flights before signing him off for combat mission. He felt comfortable to fly with me and requested to be my co-pilot for the next combat mission.

The army division received military intelligence that indicated a big enemy unit moving down to the edge of the village in the western boundary of the division control area. The operations were planned to counter, engage to stop and destroy the enemy forces as soon as possible. The US advisors at all channels were anticipating the operations for observation, advisory, and air support.

The Chinook was heavy-lift, and transport with a capacity of thirty-three fully equipped US Army troops. Since the Vietnamese soldiers were much smaller and not well armed like the US counterpart, I changed our military technical manual to increase capacity up to forty-four Vietnamese troops and described the character of the Chinook for the army commanders, making a better decision of how and when to utilize this heavy-lift transportation. However, after the briefing, I expressed my disappointment in the Army division commander to use Chinooks to transport the first company to the LZ without any assurance of the minimum ground security. Since my boss could not convince the army general of the division commander, I did not have an option to do otherwise.

Bob's advisor team leader was a one-star general US Airforce who would be flying in a Huey with my base commander, also one-star VNAF general, as the C&C (Command and Control) unit. Bob requested to fly as co-pilot with me. I had him fly with my flight leader as co-pilot, and I took the lead of the mission for the final check ride of my new training AC pilot to fill in the current open position. Bob understood the mission and his function as co-pilot of the Thien Bang Bravo. My code name was Thien Bang Alpha, the leader of a total of four Chinooks to launch a battalion army troop into the combat LZ.

All were ready to take off, but my Chinook hydraulic line busted. I lost the primary hydraulic control system. I told my Thien Bang Bravo to lead the other two Thien Bangs and report for the mission on time, and I will have the line fixed and will be in the LZ later.

I finally took off about thirty minutes after. I loaded the army troops and headed to the LZ. My Bravo reported the LZ was on sight and he was ready to land. A couple of minutes later, I lost contact with Bravo. Charlie reported Bravo got hit, believed to be SA7, on the final approach.

"Charlie, this is Alpha. Report Bravo condition," I radioed him.

"Alpha, this is Charlie, Bravo crashed and burning on the LZ, OVER."

"Charlie and Delta, do not land. Standby until the LZ cleared, OVER."

"Alpha this is Charlie, copied, do not land … Standby for further order."

I switched over the FM to contact the troops on the ground. Their radio channel was busy with a lengthy report…four soldiers died, several wounded from the fires and flames that busted out quickly, and several jumped out of the Chinook from the air and got hurt and needed to be evacuated immediately. I requested the troop leader on LZ to report my pilots' and his crew members' conditions.

I got a preliminary report, one pilot wounded severely, the loadmaster dead, and the rest were unknown. I called C&C and requested to have my downed crews to be rescued ASAP and requested the gunships come down to secure the LZ and to protect the wounded immediately.

I reported to the C&C that I was halfway to the LZ and I kept repeating it over and over on the FM radio. There were no responses or read back. The ground troops kept the FM channel very well occupied, I looked up in the sky and spotted the C&C ship at six or seven thousand feet above the ground, and the two gunships were not on the target. I then radioed to the C&C and requested permission to Thien Bang Alpha to come down to the LZ and rescue them if no one was available or willing to, without further waiting. The radio channel unexpectedly became dead silent.

I returned to the army division's pick-up point. I unloaded troops and headed to the LZ. I repeatedly radioed to all related parties that Thien Bang Alpha was ready to go down and rescue the wounded. My final report from the army troop leader on the LZ that three other crew members were found, and they were ok. I requested the gunships to secure the LZ and the ground troops to group all wounded and all crew members to be ready before I landed.

I applied the surprising tactic from KingBee to fly this giant and limited maneuverability Chinook and believed I would catch the enemy off guard.

I asked Charlie and Delta to circle in far away from the LZ and constantly monitor and report my distance to target while I came in the LZ with a longer distance at very low-level flight right on the treetops. I flared up and landed just behind the still-burning Bravo. The army troops quickly carried the wounded first and assisted my downed crew's boarding. I recognized Bob and saw him running toward my Chinook and boarding by himself and... sadly, I understood... the reported burned pilot was the flight leader, one of my close friends, and the body of his loadmaster was also brought into my Chinook.

After a couple of minutes long, I took off and flew extremely low-level, on the tree top, out of the LZ and quickly turned into a different path from which I came in. It was fast and risky, but I got out of the dangerous area instantly.

"Thien Bang Alpha, this is Sky One (code name of my big boss in C&C), OVER."

"Sky One, this is Thien Bang Alpha."

"Alpha, report the down crews' condition and the number of the ground troops wounded, OVER."

"Sky One, this is Alpha... AC wounded seriously; loadmaster ... dead, remaining are Ok. Bob is fine. Total army wounded are six; all burned seriously. Request ambulance and medic at the landing pad, Over."

I returned to the pick-up point with my other two Thien Bangs. All pilots and crew members were very nervous after learning the Bravo was shot down by SA7, the heat-seeking ground-to-air missile because our Chinooks were not equipped with flares or any other counter devices.

The operations commander then ordered the two gunships to escort three Hueys to land the assault company troop to secure the LZ first. I then led the Thien Bang Charlie and Delta to drop the rest of the battalion into the LZ and accomplished the mission in the afternoon.

Bob and I visited our wounded friends in hospitals in the earlier morning the next day. My pilot, my flight leader, got eighty percent burned and died a week later. I witnessed the deep suffering of his wife and his mother. The loadmaster's parents were also there and cried soberly for their son's death. I did not know what to say with tears in my eyes, and I felt terrible for our loss.

Bob thanked me for being brave and for saving his life and others. He respected and trusted me like his brother. Our friendship grew strongly afterward.

Ten days after the operations were accomplished, my boss told me the base commander wanted to meet me at his office. We went to the morning briefing together. The general expressed his sincere thanks for my quick and brave action to save the comrades' lives. He recognized my heroism and recommended me for a medal.

Bob invited me to his advisory team club. He introduced me to his team leader. The general tapped on my shoulder and said, "We were glad to have you. Your action on the battlefield was brave and incredible." We all had a good time and a couple of drinks.

A couple of months later, Bob introduced me to an American civilian named Brian Scott. Brian was a Boeing technician representative who was supposed to interface the chief maintenance department for information and safety updates. Since no one knew how to work with him or asked him for anything relating to the Chinook maintenance and technical updates for months, Brian wanted to move his desk to my office, next to Bob, to be more helpful. Brian said he was Boeing's employee and not in the advisory system. I liked to receive all current technical manuals (TM), and system updated information from Boeing for the safety and performance of the Chinook, so I agreed to have Brian in my office.

Unlike Bob, Brian could go anywhere without any military restriction or permit. He enjoyed Vietnamese food Linda cooked and spent more time with my family. Bob, Brian, and I worked together well and had an excellent relationship for a year.

Bob's tour was ended in a couple of days, and we three got together at the advisory club. Bob asked his boss to have permission to fly with me to Tan Son Nhut rather than taking the US Airforce C130. His team leader requested my base commander to have a depot maintenance mission to Bien Hoa instead. Brian also needed contact and coordination with the Bien Hoa Maintenance and Supply Depot. The farewell was very emotional. Bob did not want to leave me, and finally, he pulled out his notebook, wrote down his home and his father's addresses and phone numbers, and seriously asked me to call him or his father right away whenever I came to the US.

A month later, I abruptly received an order from the VNAF headquarters to be transferred to the newly formed Chinook squadron in Can Tho, south of Saigon. I had to leave my boss and my friends, with whom I had incredible relationships. Brian promised that he would request the Boeing to be transferred to Can Tho with my new 249th Chinook squadron.

My Last Air Base

The US Aviation unit had left this base in early 1973. The Vietnamese Army took over the air base security outside the defense line, but there was not much activity in the air base. One new Huey squadron just formed to provide the air support and light transport to the ground troops of the Fourth Corp.

My job was gathering and testing the left-behind Chinooks and training the pilots for the newer 249th Manh Long Chinook Squadron. Other senior pilots and I sped up the process to narrow the gap between the US aviation unit departure and new VNAF crews to provide supply and troop transport to the Vietnamese Army in this region.

Flying over the flat land area seemed safer and easier, but only for the normal condition in peace, not war. There were no mountains, no turbulence air, and no downdraft wind to deal with. In case of emergency, pilots could land anywhere because of the flat ground and smooth rice paddies spread out to the horizon.

However, you don't even assume so in this crazy war. There were very dangerous areas instead. Viet Cong was all over places with plenty of SA7s due to many good transportation networks from the ground to canals and rivers. Weather was usually very decent; the sky was blue and clear, and the lat land was wide open, which provided unobstructed target shooting from the ground.

If you could not fly at a very low-level just on top of the trees, then you better fly at least six thousand feet or higher altitude above the ground. Otherwise, you would just make yourself a clear target for antiaircraft machine guns or your aircraft would be in the perfect range for the heat-seeking ground-to-air missiles SA7. One shot and you were dead.

Most of my training missions were collecting the aircraft from many former US camps all over places, even from the center of Vietnam. Finally, my newer squadron had a total of twenty Chinooks with only a half-dozen flyable aircraft per day. The Chinook was modern and complicated aircraft which demanded very high maintenance. It required a lot of maintenance hours for every hour of flying.

In less than a year, I was promoted to Operation Officer and Vice Commander of the squadron.

Unlike others, I liked this area. The area was my dreamland. When I was young, I was hoping someday I would move to the south—the richest resource part of my country—for a better life, and here I was. The local people were laid back and enjoyed their healthy lives. There were plenty of rice, fish, fruits, and vegetables. They were available anywhere. The local weather was so nice, and the climate was just perfect. Lives were good down here except the war.

I liked to fly the support missions. I ran into many of my classmates from the National Military Academy. Many of them were battalion commanders, chiefs of districts, and many senior class members were holding the very important official keys of the military and civilian positions in the government. It was a great feeling to see them being successful in their careers.

The Firebases

The enemy kept getting closer and closer to the edges of the areas where the south government was controlling. Firebases were established for the ring and line of defense. Each base was the camp of a battalion of the army troops within an alternate support range of M105 or M155 long range artilleries. If the enemy attacked one base, then the two adjacent bases would use its artilleries to protect the middle base from being overrun by Viet Cong.

My 249th Manh Long Chinook squadron was busy supporting those bases with ammunition, food, supplies, and hauling in the heavy guns for them. The communists figured out the way to eliminate the effectiveness of M105 and M155 artilleries is to attack the firebase quickly, and they moved their soldiers closer to the last defense line where they would be out of the target areas of the supporting artilleries from other bases.

If the enemy passed the last defense line, then eventually the firebase would be overrun. Chinooks would be called in to haul off those heavy guns and ammunition out of the enemy's hands at the last minutes of the army withdrawal. The mission became very risky, and the chance to get the job done and get out alive in the last minutes was small. On the other hand, if the big guns would fall into the enemy hands, then the enemy would use those guns to wipe out the other firebases nearby, causing a domino effect to the entire security and defense lines of the whole region.

My newly formed squadron faced serious casualties from those missions and from SA7 heat-seeking missiles in the first year and a half. The squadron commander position was open while I was in Saigon headquarters for the Squadron of Staff of Commander training class, a former KingBee pilot and a Chinook pilot from Bien Hoa got promoted to fill in.

I met him during my weekend from my training class. We were very happy to be in the same unit and promised to support each other closely. The first thing I told him was "to be very careful with the dangerous flat land areas when you fly over." If he could not wait for me to return after my graduation from the Staff of Squadron (SOS) class, then I told him, "Only fly the combat missions with a flight leader who was familiar with the local battlefield first."

A week later, he got hit by the SA7 missile, and the entire crew died while I was still in my last week of the SOS class in Saigon. I returned to the squadron a couple of days after his death. Here I was again. I faced his young wife and his two little children grieving, and the families of the other four crew members. It was so painful, and I could not do anything for her, or for any of them, except I promised her to bring her husband's body and those of the others home.

It was a very tough promise, but I must deliver to her and her family as my close friend and the rest of them to their families. To the Vietnamese, after the death of a loved one, the next important thing was the dead body. They treated the body with very high respect, and they buried their loved one properly to soften their pain and suffering.

The local militants reported the Chinook was burned completely. The area was not accessible and was controlled by the enemy. I hopped in the Huey Medivac and flew into the area. The ground troop suggested to have the local farmers to guide them to the crash site, and the troops walked behind. The farmer found five bodies and the Huey Medivac came in and recovered all and loaded them up while I flew as a passenger in the Huey. The downed Chinook was just a long pile of black ash with several chunks of big metal left from engines and transmissions.

I told my friend's wife that I was very sorry for her loss and her suffering. I also lost my close friend and my brave comrade. She asked me, "Do you know for sure which body is my husband's?" because five of them were severely burned. I told her that I had made a close examination in the hospital and recognized her husband's big and long scar on the left thigh caused by the ground fire from the Special Forces operation mission with me in Laos.

She then cried very hard and passed out. Her two children cried and called "Mom... Mom..." And they both laid on her chest. They all cried... and... cried.

CH34, Choctaw helicopter

CH47, Chinook helicopter

KingBee 219 Squadron

Thien Bang 241 Squadron

Manh Long 249 Squadron

The squadron's Insignias

The author in his flight suit

ABOUT THE AUTHOR

Con Nguyen was a major in the Vietnamese Air Force. He graduated from the Vietnamese National Military Academy in 1964 and was selected to be an air force pilot student to receive several flight training classes from schools in the USA.

The author graduated as a helicopter pilot from the US, 1967. He flew CH34-Choctaw as legendary King Bee pilot for the secret missions of US Special Operations in Vietnam, Laos, Cambodia borders along the Ho Chi Minh trails from 1969-1971. He survived after two and a half years from many impossible missions serving the Special Operations.

Con Nguyen later enrolled in the Instruction Pilot course in the US for Chinook, CH47. He helped to form new Chinook squadrons and served as Instructor Pilot, Training Officer, Operations Officer, Vice Squadron Commander, and Acting Commander.

Con Nguyen escaped Viet Nam, a day after the new South Vietnamese government unconditionally surrendered on April 30, 1975.

It was a riskiest attempted escape during the country in a chaotic situation a day after American evacuated Saigon. The author traded death for life in his series of actions to do-or-die.

Fortunately, he saved not only his life but also his family and about the other 80 women and children left on the remote island Con Son in the last hours. He picked them up and flew his Chinook one-way-out without return to the Pacific Ocean and landed on USS *Okinawa* carrier at the end of April 30, 1975.

Con Nguyen is the author of the two books.

"My Last Flight Out" is an incredible long survival journey against overwhelming all odds. The story of selfless military leadership with guts, creativities, and perseverance overcame death to live. It is an extraordinary true story of the long and hard surviving journey after the war.

"My Flight To America" detailed the perilous sea survival journey on the high seas. Form the Seventh Fleet to a merchant ship, from Subic Air Base to Guam Island. His final trip was to Alaska, where the author called Anchorage his first home to resettle in America. The new lives had started in the land of freedom and opportunity for all.

With his determination and enthusiasm for venturing into new territories, he created a new life as a successful immigrant within a short time.

Thank you, the USA, for the land of freedom and opportunity.

Dear readers of *My Last Flight Out*:

By now, after you read my incredible story, you might have many questions:

What had happened next to my family and me?

Where did I go from the refugee camp?

Where have I been?

What have I been doing?

Please read **My Flight To America**

Volume 2 of *My Last Flight Out* **now is available**.

I hope you enjoy reading my complete journey.

MY FLIGHT TO AMERICA

My Last Flight Out - Volume 2

The Incredible Journey Of
A Vietnamese Refugee

CON NGUYEN

Made in the USA
Coppell, TX
04 June 2020